THE WAY OF THE
LAOWAI

THE IMPORTANCE OF INTERNATIONAL
SELF-AWARENESS FOR BUSINESS

TYLER
JOHNSON

LIONCREST
PUBLISHING

THE WAY OF THE LAOWAI
The Importance of International Self-Awareness for Businesses

ISBN   978-1-5445-0211-3 *Paperback*
        978-1-5445-0212-0 *Ebook*

For Zachary, Reese, and Carly

CONTENTS

INTRODUCTION

The China experience is so hard to put into words. Imagine these fresh first-world Americans just off the plane, stepping into a city of twenty-five million people. Two babies, no Mandarin skills, just the expectation that we were going to change the thinking of 1.4 billion people!

The China experience was like the early days of Dell in the United States: divide and conquer, except this time, in a different language. We quickly realized we didn't know what we were doing, and our model didn't work the same at all. We adapted over time and learned the culture. I recall traveling on buses stuffed with chickens to make sales calls in remote areas. Computers were delivered on bicycles.

It wasn't always easy, but building and growing businesses across Asia was a unique experience. When you didn't have resources, you just made things happen with willpower. The people across Asia turned out to be some of the most loyal and committed people...if you took the time to understand them and how they did business.

It was an experience I will never forget, one that changed me profoundly and, I believe, forever altered my view of the world for the better.

EMBRACE THE UNKNOWN

When you consider international experience and expansion as it relates to your business, what's your first reaction?

Everyone wants to see their business grow, but when most people consider the realities of kick-starting international growth, their first reaction is a mix of trepidation, confusion, and fear. While most business leaders understand on an academic level the benefits of expanding internationally, the challenges involved in fostering and leveraging international experience are intimidating.

This reaction is normal, but smart CEOs and entrepreneurs will move beyond their anxiety. They know that a massive wealth of opportunity to expand and grow in sometimes startling new directions is hiding behind their fear of the unknown. In an increasingly interconnected world, the future for many businesses lies in embracing new markets along with the cultures, experiences, and different perspectives they offer.

MY LIFE AS A LAOWAI

I know the hesitancy associated with international expansion because I've been there too. I felt that same fear and uncertainty, and I came out the other side with an entirely new perspective on international business.

In 2005 I relocated to Shanghai, China, with my family. I was sent by my employer, Dell, to help build management capability among the local employees for the company's Chinese operations. At that point, there weren't many Chinese professionals with experience in mid- and high-level management. I was directed to coach them, put new processes in place, and help them grow the business so they could eventually take over on a local level.

I was supposed to stay for two years. In the end, I stayed for ten.

Laowai (老外) is a term the Chinese use to describe a foreigner and old friend, but also an alien, an outsider to the local culture. The use of the word started in the 1980s as foreigners began to come back into China for business and resurfaced political discussions. Some people think it has a negative connotation, but personally, I think it's the perfect descriptor for what I was during my time in China.

I went through a series of phases and emotions I think many people who move or work abroad experience. When I first came to China, I was a true outsider. I arrived with an attitude and an ego: How hard could this be? I would show up, teach my colleagues what they needed to know, and that would be that.

These expectations quickly turned to frustration when met with the reality of living and working in China. Like most *laowai*, I was confronted with the deep cultural divide between the Americans and the Chinese. Everything I'd been taught about management, on both the personal and the professional side, seemed to directly oppose Chinese cultural and traditional practices. It was frustrating and confusing, and I stumbled quite a bit.

Part of the concept of the *laowai* is that no matter how much time you spend in China, and how much you try to assimilate, you will always stand out as a foreigner. You are constantly forced to examine and reexamine your preconceptions about the most basic things. You can't become Chinese, but over time, you adapt and undergo a deep and permanent change to your outlook on the world.

Eventually, I found my footing and started to assimilate to the culture in good ways and bad. I refer to extreme cases of this as "going native." I started to pick up local mannerisms and adopt more effective marketing and management techniques. I learned about the tricks, the games, and the backdoor dealings that make businesses in China tick.

Going native made it much harder to leave in the end. After a decade of living in that cultural environment, I found myself fundamentally changed. This alteration of my thought processes and mindset made it difficult to reintegrate back into US culture. Things that I previously couldn't live without just meant less. I struggled to reintegrate into American culture and found that, while I had changed, most of the people around me had stayed the same. In the US, we are often distracted by trivial, nonessential lifestyle choices—things I like to call first-world problems. Do we really need several dozen different peanut butter options at the supermarket? Or fifty cereal choices? Or this constant distraction of choice? After my time in China, I really began to weigh the difference between needs and wants.

I had made a ton of mistakes in China, but those mistakes led me to learn some major truths about international business relations. I developed an awareness of the world outside of the United States and how it works. I learned that cultural dynamics change dramatically from place to place and have massive impact on how businesses can operate. I learned international politics, systems, and hard realities of life around the world. I learned about geopolitical strategies and how to position your business to be successful, areas to avoid, and acceptance of a world that we do not control. I witnessed the power and energy of people, no matter where they came from. I learned about the dark crevasse of politics, society, and the universal troubles all countries experience.

START THINKING INTERNATIONALLY FOR YOUR BUSINESS

Before I went to China, I only knew how to do business one way. I don't have an MBA, business degree, or formal business training. Everything I had learned up to that point was through my hands-on experiences through American companies. I understood what was traditionally done but not why. My experiences abroad helped me learn not only about different cultures but about potential new business practices. I overcame this immense egotistical idea that the US knows better and does better (what some call American exceptionalism). I came back to America with many more tools in my management arsenal.

These mindset shifts and thoughts are skills you cannot

fake. I always marvel at how many companies use position titles, such as global head of marketing, global head of this or that, yet the person in that position has never lived outside the United States. I find that concerning because it means the company is not putting people in place who have the experiences necessary to foster change. The company may employ people who truly do have international experience, but they aren't utilizing them in the right roles to really make use of those skills.

The frustrating thing is that many business leaders don't even want to have the conversation about the benefits of international experience. People don't want to hear these truths for a variety of reasons. They are insecure, set in their ways, or scared of change. They are unwilling to empathize with other cultures and admit that maybe we can learn a thing or two. This is a real shame because obstinately putting your head in the sand means that you miss real opportunities to learn, grow, and improve your business and yourself.

Many large companies already have a huge presence overseas. They may or may not need to hear this message. But midsized companies that are trying to grow can't afford to ignore the opportunity to go international. If you only focus on expansion inside the US, you're limiting potential growth. There's a bigger opportunity out there in many markets across the world to test new products, find new solutions, and expand. This is specifically true in Asia, with its large populations and openness to emerging technologies.

But to leverage those markets effectively, it will be crucial to hire dual or foreign citizens who can use their experiences to work with other people across the globe.

SOFT SKILLS IN THE NEW ECONOMY

We are currently in the middle of a global technological revolution, what some call the Fourth Industrial Revolution. Businesses are abuzz over new innovations and breakthroughs in AI (artificial intelligence) driven by deep learning, the IOT (Internet of Things), which enhances productivity and a resurgence of blockchain technologies. These technologies are exciting, so it's no wonder that they dominate the conversation, but they aren't everything. What is equally important, but discussed far less, are the kinds of personal skills people will need to learn to keep companies competitive in this new economy.

Put simply, we're going to need more people with soft skills. Soft skills are personal attributes that enable someone to interact effectively and harmoniously with others. These types of soft skills are both important and rare. While everyone knows the importance of understanding technology—engineers are in massive demand right now—many underestimate the importance that people with soft skills play in a business's success.

I believe there is something very wrong with the way companies currently conduct their hiring processes. Current practices are broken and outdated, built on convenience, with limited interaction. They are potentially led by people who are incentivized purely by statistics. There is a tendency to hire by the numbers, quickly narrowing down candidates who have the correct degrees, years of experience, or use the right keywords on their résumés. We try to increase racial and gender diversity, but we ignore another diversity factor: worldliness. Situational awareness, common sense, drive, adaptability, and curiosity. People who have lived and worked abroad have a unique set of soft skills that can be far more beneficial to a growing business than another MBA.

A GUIDE FOR COMPANIES AND INDIVIDUALS

This book is for executives, founders, and chief people officers of companies who are looking to expand and don't know which direction to go in. It's also for those who know they want to take their business to the next level but can't figure out how to get there because they haven't hired the right people, and they don't know where to find new talent or how to unleash their current talent.

Many organizations have tried to automate processes for convenience, but you can't automate personalities. It's important to make a personal connection with employees to truly understand their strengths. Leaders tend to hire people with very similar experiences and then bemoan the fact that they aren't getting different results. This book aims to help you grow and change your company in a new direction. I believe that having this sort of international awareness can truly change a company for the better on many levels.

This book is also for individuals who want to learn and grow, and who believe that an international perspective might help them to get where they are trying to go.

THE EIGHT LESSONS

In the next eight chapters, I will present eight compelling arguments for international expansion. I will share some of the key knowledge I took away from over a decade abroad. I've distilled my wealth of experiences into eight major truths about international business that can help strengthen and guide your company.

Not all my experiences were glamorous, and I had to learn many things the hard way. Some of my stories may be funny, and some may be shocking, but they all contribute to an understanding of larger cultural truths.

There are also stories so out there that I still can't really share them.

Some of these concepts are difficult for people to understand unless they have lived abroad and learned them firsthand. While it's one thing to read these stories on paper, it is quite another to experience them. Note, too, that while my personal experience was in China and some other parts of Asia, I believe these lessons transcend China and can be learned and understood from living abroad almost anywhere. No matter what country you go to, your degree of cultural awareness will dictate how you are able to do business there.

I would like this book to serve as a model for the kind of personal growth and soft skills development that arise from doing business in a culturally connected world. I also hope to reduce some of the fear and anxiety that arises around doing business overseas. I want to encourage the creation of programs within companies that foster and recognize international experience, awareness, and mindset shift. Throughout these lessons, I will also offer some prescriptive advice on how you can tweak your international programs to make them more effective.

My goal is to encourage you to move beyond fear of the unknown, to demystify some of the issues surrounding international business relations, and to encourage you to

embrace and foster international connections to improve
and move your business forward.

LESSON 1

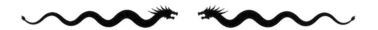

THE WORLD IS BIGGER THAN YOU

Two-thirds of the population of the entire world lives in Asia. That's nearly 4.5 billion people as of 2018,[1] with over 35 percent of the world's population living in China or India.[2] In China, there are over a hundred cities with more than a million people in them and at least fifteen cities with over ten million residents. In comparison, the United States has only ten cities larger than a million people and no cities with over ten million people.[3]

---

1   "Asia Population," Worldometers, accessed December 15, 2018, http://www.worldometers. info/world-population/asia-population/.

2   Conrad Hackett, "Which 7 Countries Hold Half the World's Population?" Pew Research Center, July 11, 2018, http://www.pewresearch.org/fact-tank/2018/07/11/world-population-day/.

3   Joe Myers, "You Knew China's Cities Were Growing. But the Real Numbers Are Stunning," World Economic Forum, June 20,2015, https://www.weforum.org/agenda/2016/06/ china-cities-growing-numbers-are-stunning/.

The scope of economic growth in China alone is incredible. In 1981, 88 percent of China's population was below the poverty line. In 2018, it's less than 2 percent.[4] In less than forty years, over eight hundred million people in China have lifted themselves out of poverty.[5] That's over two times the total population of the United States. This is a remarkable feat that will probably never be replicated again in our lifetimes.

As you can see, the United States is just a small part of a much larger economic picture. The entire world has an estimated debt of $200 trillion[6] (the exact number is hard to pin down due to shadow banking, lack of transparency in many countries, and how "debt" is truly calculated). The United States, despite being the largest economy in the world, possesses anywhere from 10 to 20 percent of that debt, depending on how you calculate. Yes, we are a major player, but we are only one of many, and this highlights the extreme pace of growth across the world.

Over the course of my career, people have asked me many questions about working in Asia, such as "What part of Japan is Hong Kong in?" At first, I was shocked by their

---

4   "The World Bank in China: Overview," The World Bank, last updated September 26, 2018, https://www.worldbank.org/en/country/china/overview.

5   Ibid.

6   "Visualizing Global Debt," McKinsey & Company, last updated June 2018, https://www.mckinsey.com/business-functions/strategy-and-corporate-finance/our-insights/visualizing-global-debt.

ignorance, but over time, I have come to realize that many people have no idea about the scope of the world, much less basic geography.

There are roughly 196 countries in the world, and close to eight billion people. That's a lot to wrap your brain around. Each of these countries is complex in its own way. They sometimes share similarities, but they each have their own culture and characteristics, their own borders and relationships. In every location you want to do business in, you need a grasp of these particulars. In each place, business needs to be conducted differently.

The world is big and full of opportunities if you can keep your perceptions in check.

A SHIFT IN PERSPECTIVE

China is made up of thirty-two provinces, or some people say divisions, just like the US has fifty states, but the population is much larger for each province in China. With continued migration to the cities, by around 2030 the largest cities on the coast will exceed fifty million people each. Infrastructure is now being completed to connect some of these megacities into "super cities" of 120 million people or more. The connections between the southern cities of Hong Kong, Shenzhen, and Guangzhou have already been completed.

My initial job in China with Dell was to shadow local leaders and "teach" them how sales management works. This still makes me laugh. I was the one being taught. About halfway through my tenure in China, I led the professional services organization for Asia. This included all IT infrastructure professional service: PC help desks, data center design/management, cloud migration, and business process operations. Simply put, we sold people's time with some tools to manage their business.

My team had the opportunity to sell one of these large service contracts to a banking-related state-owned enterprise (SOE). We went to them to speak about the best practices for automating their bank transactions and the additional technology we could provide to help with that. After we finished our detailed pitch, the client quickly came back to us and said, "I don't think you guys understand what we need."

At that time, I had a pretty big ego and couldn't fathom the rejection. Why didn't they understand the unique opportunity to partner with an American company? Did they not see the opportunity my colleagues and I were offering them?

Once they began to explain the number of transactions that they do in their province daily, my jaw dropped. They did more banking transactions in this one province than the entire United States does in one day. They didn't believe our system could handle that, and I thought they were probably right. We needed to start smaller.

Our pitch ended up failing because we couldn't support that province's needs, but my perspective on the world changed in an instant. This was a lesson on the size of the world outside America. I didn't understand the scope of what I was dealing with because I had never encountered it before.

That pitch sent us into a bit of a panic, but we regrouped, and that anxiety turned into excitement. There was a pervasive feeling of "Oh god, we're going to need a bigger boat!" This whole enterprise was a lot bigger than we'd anticipated, and we would have to rethink our approach.

THE CHALLENGES OF BIG POPULATIONS

In 2006 I frequently traveled domestically in China for work. Once, I was on my way home to Shanghai when I got stuck at the very crowded Shenzhen airport. There were delays, and the crowd was extremely frustrated. The gate was packed with people, shoulder to shoulder. One guy in particular was causing a stir. Suddenly, a fight broke out, and that passenger took a swing at the female gate agent. People were pulling them apart, and others in the crowd began to get involved separating them. I looked for the exits, but the area was so crowded there was no chance of escape. All I could think was "Where are the police?"

After what seemed like an eternity, but was probably a few minutes, guards appeared. Instead of going after the rowdy passenger, they took the ticket agent away. The customer who had instigated the brawl got back in line and boarded his plane.

I was astounded. In America, a passenger who attacked a gate agent like that would have been arrested. Instead, he was just allowed to go on his way. It seemed crazy to me, but in China, it's just crowd control. Security got there late. The guy who'd started the fight had the crowd on his side. The guards had to pacify the crowd or risk starting a riot they would be unable to control. So they took the path of least resistance to defuse the conflict.

China has a long history of walking the balance between controlling the population and preventing uprisings. There are just so many people that there is no way to control all of them. My experience at the airport really illustrated how important it is for the government to keep things in line using methods other than force. This includes strictly controlling the media and flow of information to the people. The sheer amount of people in China makes it difficult to keep everyone happy. Managing and maintaining control can be difficult, and communication and information are critical.

ON-THE-GROUND EXPERIENCE

India and China are both huge markets that companies are very eager to tap into. On occasion, I would be in India when Dell executives from the US or Europe came to try to understand the business environment there a little better. This was code for telling us what to do, because they obviously knew best. I once drove from the airport to the office in Bangalore with one of these executives. We had to go through a series of tollbooths along the way. The executive couldn't understand why there were still people manually taking tickets in each booth when the process could be so easily automated. He wanted to know why we weren't jumping at this enormous opportunity to sell our technology.

What the exec didn't understand were the economic realities of life in India. Each of these tollbooth operators only made around one US dollar a day. Why would the city invest millions of dollars on a solution they didn't need when they could pay ten guys to collect tolls for nearly nothing?

When he realized the situation, you could practically see

a light bulb go off above his head. He finally got how complicated the local environment could be. After that, the Dell home office stopped insisting we push that particular service and started looking for other ways to break into the market.

You can't manage from afar without understanding the dynamics at play on the ground. Sometimes you really need to be there, in that foreign place, to see for yourself. These moments of deep understanding are extremely helpful because they allow you to pivot and develop unique products and services that best suit the market you are trying to break into.

MAJOR TAKEAWAYS

The world is only as big as you make it. Be curious and open-minded so that you can take advantage of the many opportunities out there.

AN EXPANSIVE MARKET

The sheer size of the markets in the East means that there is a nearly endless wealth of opportunity. The implications for businesses are huge.

In China, you don't have to go after the whole market; you can find niches within which you can be extremely successful. Just 1 percent of market share in China is a huge number.

SOLUTIONS TAILORED TO SPECIFICS

In developed markets, businesses are trying to fit into a market where the average spend is much higher. It might be more challenging to sell a $5,000 computer in Asia, where average incomes are lower, so there needs to be room for adaptation and adjustment to local markets.

Developed markets tend to have ingrained practices when it comes to products and services. In Asia, there is a lot more room for variation and improvisation. In these emerging markets, you can test services more easily as you tailor solutions to the people you are selling to. Yes, it's a more competitive market. This is good. Follow the money.

KEEP AN EYE ON INCREASING PROSPERITY

In order to put a measurement on the future potential of the Chinese customer base, our company tracked per capita income in China compared to the rest of the world. Developed countries tend to spend a lot because they make a lot. The US per capita income is roughly $58,000 USD, compared to China's $8,000. That seems very small, but consider this: in 1990, China's per capita income was around $350. At this rate, by 2025 it could be $18,000.

With this rapid growth in wealth comes rapid spending. Back in 2005, I remember trying to imagine what China would look like in ten years. Today the Chinese are opening more bank accounts and buying more cars than ever. There are more Porsches, Ferraris, and Bentleys on the road there than you'll ever see in the US. There are only three ways for Chinese nationals to spend money legally: buy local stocks, buy real estate, or spend their money locally.

As companies look to grow in certain areas, they should follow the money. An increase in prosperity for consumers is going to translate into massive spending increases. It's simple logic that the more people make, the more they are going to spend. This opens a wealth of opportunities. The average person in China saves somewhere around 50 percent of their income, compared to the US citizen's 1 percent average savings. Now, imagine how much money would flood the market if that 50 percent savings went down to 25 percent.

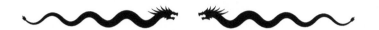

HISTORY SHAPES CULTURE; CULTURE SHAPES LEADERSHIP

Though it's hard to comprehend, China has existed in some form or another for over five thousand years. It has been through thirteen dynasties, or twenty-five if you count the different warring factions. Most of those dynasties lasted for hundreds of years. The last dynasty of China, the Qing dynasty, lasted over 276 years. That's longer than the US has even been a country!

In the last two centuries, China has been torn apart, been put back together, become a world GDP leader, and survived a handful of wars, famines, and some of the largest natural disasters in history. More recently, they have pulled over eight hundred million out of poverty while on the brink of changing the global technology landscape.

An interesting nuance that I witnessed during my time in China had to do with geography and historical bad blood between people from different regions. For example, I learned that it was difficult to pair mainland Chinese with people from Hong Kong or Taiwan. Staff from Shanghai and others from Beijing would frequently get into arguments. As a result, it was easier to assign Shanghainese salespeople to get things done in Shanghai, regardless of their skillsets, and assign Beijing employees to their own city.

If you understand a culture and where people come from, their education, their politics, and their history, you're more likely to connect, empathize, and motivate them. It's not only true in China but in other countries as well, including the US. Understanding the nuances that come along with culture is incredibly important for people to be successful in business and interpersonal relationships.

CLASHING IDEAS

Early on in my time in China, I experienced a lot of misunderstandings and clashes with the local community of people that worked for me. Part of the conflict was due to my own ego and my belief that I knew the best way to do things, despite being transplanted into an entirely new culture. Time and time again, I'd find myself having trouble managing my employees. Instead of viewing their unique insights as a valuable resource, I wouldn't listen to their advice. I ignored them when they told me certain strategies wouldn't work. I just kept pushing and pushing without understanding the cultural differences until I eventually failed. People left because of me. They didn't want to work for our company until we changed our model and our way of thinking.

To be fair, some of these cultural differences were very difficult to wrap your head around. I remember when the weather turned cold and all the Westerners couldn't understand why the heat wasn't turned on in the building. Imagine us wearing hats, gloves, and jackets inside, trying to type at our computers. We later learned that below a certain latitude in China, buildings don't have heat. Even in locations where they do, the heat is only turned on after a certain date, no matter the weather.

I wasn't used to the rigid nature of the government rules. I had been evaluating the situation based on the preconceptions I'd grown up with in the US, which may as well have been a completely different planet. It made me take a hard look at the country I was now living in. Is this how my employees had grown up? Did they have heat in their houses? Did they burn coal? What's the history behind that? What are the implications?

It took me years to finally understand the cultural issues I was dealing with. Eventually, I could attract more people by changing my business strategies and better respecting the culture. Building that trust took time, but it worked.

CULTURAL UNDERSTANDING IN MANAGEMENT

Education is a very important cultural marker to understand when it comes to managing people. The Chinese education system is very rigorous, with strict rules and an emphasis on science, technology, and math. Typically, it doesn't allow a lot of room for creativity or independence outside of government-driven policies.

In the US school system, we emphasize the finished result over the process. This translates into how we manage employees as well. When assigning a task, you might simply give your employee a goal and leave it up to them to decide how they want to achieve it. This doesn't work in China. Instead, when assigning a task, you need to list out the ten steps they need to do to complete the assignment. Your employee then follows each of the steps one by one.

In Japan, our team ran into similar cultural issues. Organizations in Japan have a strong team-driven mentality with very little emphasis on individuality. When trying to motivate workers, it's essential to motivate the whole team, not just a few individuals. Even if one individual is quite successful, if the team fails, that is considered a failure. Understanding this is essential for adapting to communication and management styles in Japan.

Management styles are also affected by China's political history. Years of political clashes and dynasties have brought forth rulers all espousing the right way for people to think, act, and live. Many books have been written about the different leadership philosophies espoused by China's leaders, including, most recently, Mao Zedong and Deng Xiaoping. Business leaders may try to emulate their leadership styles.

The same applies to religion. China does not officially recognize religions, but philosophically there's a mix of Confucianism, Taoism, and Buddhism. These ideologies have interacted over thousands of years. Religious belief systems will help determine people's ideas and how they think. Interactions with them can be nuanced in ways that play on these perceptions. If you understand the core concepts and ideologies around Buddhism or Taoism, then you will be able to connect with certain people more effectively.

Developing a deep understating of this historical and

cultural backdrop improves your ability to lead individuals in the specific environment. With this knowledge, you can develop solutions and management approaches that better fit the people and environment you must work within.

ADAPTING NEW BUSINESS STRATEGIES

When I moved to China in 2005, Dell was primarily a direct-selling engine: we sold computers directly to businesses and individuals. This made the company very popular back in the United States because it cut out the resellers as middlemen. It was a new way of selling computers, and it revolutionized the industry.

This model, which thrived in the West, didn't work very well in China. While we had the supply chain worked out, Dell made very little headway with the direct sales model. Eventually, we had to abandon it completely. Part of the reason was that Dell didn't understand the way business is conducted in China. Deals are made through backdoor channels with private dealings and often payoffs for multiple parties. There is always heightened risk in business with multiple channels, retail partners, and third-party involvement. Adapt or die.

In the earlier days, Dell (and most foreign companies) didn't want to do business that way and pushed back.

As a result, the company lost market share, as did many other companies who were forced to change and adapt. The indirect business model in China has had a strong influence in shaping future business models across the world. A multitiered and channel-driven sales model was right for China. Today, the majority of Dell's business worldwide is driven through channels, partners, and distribution models.

We were naïve to think we could come in and push our choice of model for doing business in China. Hundreds of years of business history simply can't be altered overnight. We learned, painfully, that we had to adapt to survive.

THE ROLE OF GOVERNMENT IN BUSINESS

The Chinese approach to business is strongly colored by the fact that almost all major domestic companies have either evolved from state-owned enterprises or have emerged as competition against those SOEs. In the last ten years, a new wave of technology companies has altered the role of private companies in China. Many of the first new age tech companies like Alibaba, Tencent, and Baidu are listed on foreign and domestic stock exchanges. They are hybrids: they are not part of the government, but they still work closely with the government and help to drive government initiatives. They have a role to play in the broader spectrum of the country's economic goals by helping to move along technological advances and society. You could say technology forced the government to embrace change, or some may say technology was the tool used by the government to accelerate change.

For decades, the Chinese government had complete control over the domestic economy, and nearly all companies were state-owned enterprises. Typically, these state-owned entities rotated their leadership among party members. Executives would move from China Unicom to China Telecom to an oil-and-gas firm (picture red phones in their offices for direct lines to the "powers"). These leaders weren't always well-versed in the specific industry they were appointed to and always needed to report back to the state.

Over the course of the last twenty years, the business sector has started to detach from the state in many ways, with increased competition and the appearance of new and foreign companies. However, the government still exercises heavy control over how businesses can operate. China has been very successful using an "experimentation" model to drive, test, and implement change inside and outside China.

The government dictates laws based on the way they want businesses to behave. For example, when they rolled out 4G service across mobile platforms, businesses were "awarded" licenses to offer the service. The government dictated who received a portion of the licenses in each province. All state-owned telecommunication firms got a certain number, as did certain large, well-established companies. Companies on the lower rungs of the ladder might only get three licenses while those at the top would get fifteen.

This kind of regulation put the emphasis less on competing with other businesses on a consumer level and more on maintaining favor with the government. It isn't an open system, and there is a real lack of transparency as to how the government makes decisions.

Over the past decade, this lack of transparency has been challenged by advances in technology, but the influence of the politics is still very important to consider when planning your business strategy. Understanding who is connected to whom and how some people might fit into certain business dynamics could influence how you assign staff to certain projects, regardless of skillsets. Sometimes it's just about someone's connections or having the right name attached to your application.

It's also very important to be aware of the dark underbelly of the way government and business interact in China and in most countries in the world. There is corruption everywhere. There are two layers to how things get done:

the surface layer that people see and the way things really get done. Most effective business transactions are negotiated through back channels, personal relations, or family relationships, some of which stretch back hundreds of years. Unfortunately, an element of organized crime is also sometimes involved.

This lack of openness, still prevalent in society, is one of the hurdles that the Chinese must overcome as they continue to become more involved in the global business world.

THE IMPORTANCE OF SYMBOLISM

Compared to China, the US is a very young country. In fact, most countries in Asia, and around the world, have existed far longer than America. To connect and effectively do business with people from these countries, you need to respect their cultural seniority.

Denying other cultures this admiration, especially in China, is like a punk kid telling an adult that they know best. It's disrespectful and can get in the way of making a meaningful business connection. You need to respect the people and their process of getting things done.

An important theme that's developed through the course of China's long history is the importance of symbolism. In

Chinese culture, there is a deep awareness of the meaning of various symbols, and these influence personal behavior as well as business.

When I first arrived in China, I was unaware of these symbols and, in some cases, brushed them off. In retrospect, I was very close-minded in my view of the world. I didn't realize how deep some of these symbols run and how uniformly people adhere to their meanings.

In the US, we don't really have potent business symbolism. The beliefs we do have sometimes directly contradict expected behavior in Asia. For example, in the US we assign a lot of importance to looking people in the eye and giving them a firm handshake. It gives the impression of strength and trustworthiness. In many Asian countries, this gesture may be meaningless or even considered aggressive or rude. Even in a very Westernized country like Singapore, you are expected to look down and away if you've done something wrong. You are not supposed to make eye contact. This is a sign of respect.

In Japan, there is a lot of symbolism assigned to bowing in business culture. The angle, the length of time, and how far down you go all have significant meaning. The lower you bow, the more respect you have for that individual. Early on, I made the mistake of running up to some

Japanese higher-ups and trying to shake their hands. As it turned out, getting in their face was not appreciated.

Being a Westerner, you are usually allowed a little leeway, but if you know these things up front, you'll receive much more respect from other people.

LITTLE DETAILS, BIG MEANING

Business meetings in Asia are often completely unlike what we are used to. In the US, the purpose of most meetings is to conduct negotiations. In Asia, all negotiations are done through back channels. The meeting itself is often just a symbolic rubber stamp to reinforce a relationship or to give face or credit to certain people. The signing of a contract, for example, doesn't hinge on the scheduled meeting; the meeting is more of a gesture to formalize the successful deal. As a result, there are a lot of small details that need to be carefully considered, including what you wear. Red is always a good choice in China, as it's a symbol of good fortune.

Where you sit in a US business meeting is usually arbitrary, but in China and other Asian countries, people are carefully seated according to their power within the company. Dictating who sits where is also a power move, a way to put yourself on equal footing with someone else. If your title was Vice President of Asian Markets and you were meeting with somebody at a high level, you'd want to be seated directly across from them. At banquets, the same would be true. Seating to the left or right is meaningful, depending on the seniority and power of the individual. The power seat at dinners is seated facing the door.

Finally, there's a lot of symbolism around exchanging gifts or items. In the US, you don't typically take gifts into meetings at all. In Asian cultures, particularly China and Japan, gifts are expected, and they matter quite a bit. For example, you never want to give a watch to anyone because it symbolizes someone's time is up—death.

The Chinese are superstitious and put a lot of faith in lucky numbers and the Chinese zodiac signs. Each sign comes around every twelve years. When my son was born in China in 2007, he was a "golden pig," a sign that only occurs every sixty years! As a result, he was showered with praise and gifts, as it was believed that the good luck would rub off on the giver. Numbers are equally important in guiding the psyche. The lucky number eight is in constant use, from mobile phone numbers to pricing levels for merchandise. I will be forever driven by the luck of the zodiac and numbers. I'm a believer.

The gifts that go over well tend to appeal to a person's personality or culture. For example, I'm from Texas, so if I were to bring barbecue sauce as a gift, that would be meaningful and appreciated. Many people have preconceived ideas about Texas and may have heard of Texas barbecue. I would come across as an ambassador for my culture. Conversely, it would also be appropriate to show an understanding of the host's culture and appeal to that, like bringing sake or whiskey to a Japanese person.

These gestures all have significant meaning. Learning and acquiescing to symbolism shows that you have taken the time to understand another culture rather than just coming in, making a deal, and leaving. It typically takes much longer to build relationships in Asian cultures compared to the Western world, but a little bit of effort can really help facilitate the process.

MAJOR TAKEAWAYS

Paying attention to the small details of symbolism and cultural norms transformed my worldview. Living and working in Asia for ten years wound up changing my entire perspective. My situational awareness was enhanced.

TAKE THE LESSONS HOME

When I came back to the US, it was difficult to reintegrate. But I noticed that my attention to detail and observations of people and their actions were more acute. I was more aware of others, how they acted, what they wore, what they ate, what they said, and how they communicated. Although my China-specific knowledge is not as useful working in the States, the cultural observation skills I learned are.

REDEFINE TALENT WHEN HIRING

As I have integrated back into the US business world and culture, it has become clear to me that current hiring processes are not sufficient. Today, I advise hiring managers to look for people with a diversity of international experiences over specific skillsets, gender, and racial diversity. The international experience brings different viewpoints and ways of adapting to the table.

Over the next five to ten years, companies need to start robust rotation programs that allow individuals to move to other countries and experience more, whether in Europe, the Middle East, or Asia. It will allow individuals to grow and adopt different ways of thinking. It will put people in situations where they must adapt, which is very important for business leaders and those looking to be in leadership roles. Comfort is not your friend if you want to grow personally and professionally.

A great example of this is the US military. They do an unbelievable job of rotating individuals within their organization to pick up new skills and tasks. They typically move people every two to three years. They put them in roles they are not completely comfortable in and train them. What they end up with are very well-rounded individuals who can step into a more diverse type of role or career.

Companies should also reconsider the timeline of international assignments. Six months is not enough time to really acclimate to a new culture. Two years may not even be enough. For someone to truly understand what is going on in another culture and for them to learn to adapt in uncomfortable situations takes a lot of time. After ten years in China, I still don't understand all there is, but I learned a lot.

BE PROACTIVE WHEN ABROAD

Part of living abroad and adapting is asking a lot of questions, the right way, in order to build trust. The more questions you ask, the more you will understand why things are done. Too often, not asking about the meanings of symbols, policies, government practices, and histories hobbles people. If I were to do it all over again, I would try to go with an open mind and a mouthful of questions so that I could get the context earlier for how people do things and how business works.

When working abroad it's very important to learn some

of the language, even if it's just a few phrases. It doesn't matter if your pronunciation is bad. Understanding language can go a long way in helping you get along and show respect to the people you're speaking to.

It's also important to try to understand food culture. Food plays an incredibly important role in cultural dynamics, particularly in Asia. Showing proper respect for the food is super important. You should try everything at least once. Even if you don't like it, that's okay; just trying shows your respect. At banquets and business dinners, I would always try to eat local food. Some individuals, even executives, would come in from other countries and refuse to even try anything new. It sent a signal that they didn't care and that they weren't open to a relationship.

THE UNDERBELLY OF INFORMAL NETWORKS

All countries have an underbelly. There are businesses that are known to be owned and operated by families or organizations who have connections to the mafia or organized crime families. These lines of distinction between government, crimes families, and day-to-day criminals are often blurred. The government even recognizes them in some cases, such as the Yakuza in Japan. In China, you have the Triad. In Russia, the Vory. We can't ignore that these dynamics exist and must be recognized. If you're going to do business in some cultures, it's just how things are done. If you are looking for fairness and legal systems that support true justice, think again. What happens on the surface is likely not reality.

Doing business in other countries often involves understanding the underbelly of informal networks. How you effectively maneuver these obstacles and challenges and turn them into opportunities will ultimately help you shine as a leader. To get things done in China, I had to understand these particular dynamics.

LESSON 3

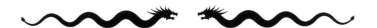

PLANNING FOR CREATIVITY

Most Westerners believe that China is not a very creative place. Before I went to China, I had the same perception. I thought the people weren't very creative because of what I knew about their authoritarian government and collective culture. I was wrong.

The truth is that if you look at China's history, they are responsible for many world-changing innovations, including gunpowder, paper, and iron ore. This may be referred to in Chinese as *Youchuangzaoli De (*有创造力的*)*, which refers to the Chinese people's innate drive to innovate throughout history or having creativity. The people of China have always had a can-do attitude. If they don't know how to make something work, give them enough time, and they will figure it out. Part of this mentality and creativity is driven by the rules and regulations inside the country, which create the need for innovative problem-solving. There is an immense drive and determination to be successful.

This confident attitude is reflected in China's policies over the last ten years. While most people perceive the Chinese government as ultra-authoritarian, they truthfully have a pretty unique process to foster nationwide change. They experiment with different ways of doing things. Some work and others don't, but that's okay. They build on the experiments that don't work and tinker with them until they become more effective and beneficial for society.

GOVERNMENT-DRIVEN CREATIVITY

As in many Western countries, the government in China is a driving force for innovation. They do this by treating each of the thirty-three provinces/divisions as its own company. From 2000 to 2016, an era of high growth, the central government provided GDP targets for each province. It was a controlled push for them to be successful. If they hit 7 percent or 10 percent growth, they were rewarded with resources, government grants and loans, praise, and promotions. Annual GDP growth in some years exceeded 12 percent!

This competition among provinces led to a lot of creative

strategies to pull ahead, such as the creation of special economic zones (SEZ). SEZs are areas with special rules for trade, invention, and commerce that allow for more "flexible laws."

The current day's government initiatives tend to center around automation, digital transformation, and technology leadership for advancing military, healthcare, and global leadership. For example, the government has certain provinces testing automation technologies that help manage and distribute healthcare more effectively. Different provinces are testing different models for efficiency and viability. New technology companies are enhancing ways to distribute pharmaceuticals, cut out inefficiencies, and provide medications to critically ill patients who lack the means to quickly get much-needed assistance. Based on what they discover, they may pivot their national strategy.

To accomplish this, the government gives a lot of autonomy to agencies, as well as low-interest or long-dated loans that agencies don't have to pay back for forty or fifty years. Even though these agencies have a lot of freedom and are even allowed to fail, the government is testing new concepts in a controlled area. In the US, we have a version of this for startups on platforms funded by venture capital firms. The difference between the US and China lies in how the money flows and who supports the companies. In China, the government controls a company's flow within the initiatives of the state and their planned society. Or they might be controlled by private VC firms that are nonetheless dedicated to driving state initiatives. The question mark for the Western world lies in the flow of money to support new and emerging businesses. Is China serious this time versus their past efforts to "change"? There is a constant cloud around the flow of money and who controls the end point.

The same applies to the free-trade zones China has on the coast, where companies follow alternative government laws or regulations. They allow foreign companies to set up there and do business externally and internally. It's almost like having another country within these zones. But really, they are all testing out certain business models, trade policies, and regulations.

Today, many of China's internal infrastructure and technological goals have been realized, and they are turning their ambitions outward toward global expansion. In 2013, they launched the One Belt, One Road plan with the aim of reestablishing a modern-day Silk Road by enhancing trade, technology, and culture across over sixty countries and 65 percent of the world's population. They are supporting new trade routes, infrastructure, and financing abroad through the Asia Infrastructure Investment Bank (AIIB).

This is a highly debated initiative in the geopolitical world. Will it work? Is it overly ambitious? Is it just a means for control? What are the government's motives? Controversy aside, it's a great example of China's current global mindset.

COMPETITION AND COLLABORATION

In the past, if a foreign company wanted to set up shop in China, it had to be a joint venture. Certain industries, including car manufacturing, banking, and insurance, were highly regulated. Over the last twenty years or so, the percentages of allowable foreign ownership inside a company have increased and decreased depending on the "readiness" of the market, as set forth by the government. There were only a handful of industries where foreign companies could be wholly owned.

This meant that car manufacturers like Ford, GM, Toyota, and Volkswagen had to set up joint ventures with local car manufacturers inside of China if they wanted to do business. Siemens had over seventy joint ventures across China. The local car companies benefited greatly from this partnership system, as they had the opportunity to learn from some of the biggest companies in the world. The major drawback to this system, from a foreign perspective, is an underlying concern over intellectual property–related transfer. Who owns the IP created by the joint companies? Is it one-sided?

Doing business in China means following steps as dictated by the government. It's done that way to protect the interests of the country and to help the local market innovate. Many countries have done this to some degree, depending on where they are in the maturation of the economy. Many unique products come out of these joint ventures, such as car manufacturers creating localized versions of specific vehicles.

In India, foreign companies are often forced to adapt and partner with local businesses. Most people there can't afford a $25,000 car, so a lot of firms have figured out how to restructure and manufacture cars to sell for under $1,000 to $2,000. The same happens with farm equipment manufacturers like Caterpillar and John Deere. Even competitors have struck up unlikely partnerships in China, with internet firms like Baidu teaming up with Google. These kinds of collaborations don't happen in developed countries due to the more competitive dynamic and/or a resistance to trying something different.

Sometimes a market catalyst can accelerate change and competition. A good example of this is the e-commerce battle currently going on in India. Walmart recently bought Flipkart, India's biggest online store, while Amazon has partnered with local companies, and Alibaba has invested in several key e-commerce and cashless payment companies. The competition between these foreign companies works to build the local economy and creates more and better options for the Indian people.

This partnering of companies and experimentation drives a lot of creativity and innovation. It's an interesting dynamic that is facilitated and controlled by the government, but it still yields results.

THE ADVANTAGE OF STARTING FROM ZERO

One of the reasons China and other emerging markets can leapfrog right into testing new technologies is because they have limited legacy systems. They are adopting systems from whole cloth, not replacing outdated ones. In most cases, they are purely driven to improve society.

In the US, we've been doing business for a while. A lot of manufacturing and financial firms operate on software that has been created or adopted specifically to make it run. With these legacy structures in place, it's hard to move on to the next technology. In emerging markets, it's easier to skip ahead to the most current technology.

In the past, people in America used to write checks and mail them to pay bills. China never had checks. They leapfrogged right into online payments and cashless technology, innovations like face recognition for payments, fingerprints at immigration, and bar codes for merchandising. Now, they lead the world in online transactions. We are just now adopting this technology in the US. Hong Kong was doing fingerprint immigration entry ten years ago; the US is just now starting to adopt some form of this.

In the United States, we have developed a lot of great processes and procedures for managing people and businesses, but the Chinese often find ways to improve on them. A good example of this is sales forecasting data. US sales forecasting, while being detailed, doesn't get into the excruciating finer points and complexity, including multiple spheres of influence for partners, financial considerations, government influence, and increased competition. In the US, we are always trying to simplify things. The Chinese don't simplify. They have a lot of different pieces to consider: personal interests, business interests, government interests, and outside influences. You could say, the Chinese are patient...until they are not and want to do a quick deal.

FILLING IN THE KNOWLEDGE GAPS

The Chinese are very good at a lot of things, including admitting when they don't have expertise in a certain area. To save face, they won't tell you directly that they don't know something, but they are driven to figure things out, and that unquenchable drive for success typically wins in the end. Conversely, they are also very skilled at not letting on when they really know much more than they want you to think.

Twenty years ago, China let foreigners into the country specifically to address tech and management expertise they were lacking. They wanted to learn how to manage in a corporate environment and lead in a multinational way. Today, they still use initiatives to attract foreign individuals and businesses that have certain skills or expertise that align with government goals.

A good example is in the realm of computer-chip making. The Chinese needed to develop their capabilities, so they actively invited PhDs and engineers to come help with the development of people and industries. They used tax incentives and state pensions (available to those who stay for twenty or more years) to entice new talent.

In 2005 many Chinese businesses had limited management processes in place. They didn't do management reviews or personal evaluations because, historically, you landed and kept your job because of who you knew, not your personal skills. Today, there are more systems in place, such as HR departments, ethics departments, and full boards for listed and non-listed companies, although it's debatable how effective they are. On the flip side, you could say the same for many Western organizations, the difference again being the transparency and enforcement of law.

By 2025, China wants to be a leader in AI. They know they aren't at the forefront in some areas, so they have a plan to build those skills by importing new talent. Arguably, they are ahead in many areas. Data is the new oil. With 1.4 billion people, there is plenty of data in China. With limited enforcement of privacy laws and the use of AI to control society, this raises some ethical questions about what governments should and shouldn't be able to do with this new technology. The same is true for some of the largest Western tech companies in the world. This will be a big topic in the years and decades to come.

The Chinese are great at honestly examining their weaknesses and addressing them head-on. Their unique system for constant improvement, individual drive, and innovation begs the question of whether a planned economy or a free economy is better.

THE DOWNSIDE OF STATE-FOSTERED CREATIVITY

There is a lot of emphasis on moving the society forward in China. Because of this, with planned societies, there's always an opening for corruption. People fudge numbers and doctor books. There's a lot of waste because money isn't an issue if the end results are achieved. Basically, businesses are not worried about what they ruin in their journey to success. You see this with the limited enforcement of laws or regulations around the environment. Pollution, deforestation, and "greening" the country are major priorities for the Chinese, and many experiments are currently in play to help improve the environment. Time will tell of their effectiveness.

China isn't alone in this issue. The US has been guilty of a lot of these sins as well, particularly in earlier stages of development. China is bigger and growing faster, so its negative by-products are three- or fourfold what a smaller country might output.

There's a lot of fraud in China too. Whereas in the US we use personal signatures, they have something called "the chop" where official documents must be chopped with an official seal. A lot of these chops are altered or falsified to forge approvals. You also see it today with IP issues. A lot of companies claim that China is stealing their secrets, and there is probably some legitimacy to those claims. Maybe blockchain technology will change this in the future.

In addition to intellectual theft, there are cases of outright plagiarism or brand infringement. There are knockoff copies of famous landmark brands everywhere in China. You'll run into an Eiffel Tower in the middle of a town or a brand name that is just one letter off from another very well-known one. On the street, you can buy the latest movies for a buck, computer software for five dollars.

From a consumer standpoint, it was glorious. Imagine five-dollar children's Nikes that lasted just long enough for your child to grow out of them. Before 2008, my family and I filled suitcases of consumer goods to bring back to the United States with us because everything was cheaper in China. After the 2008 financial crisis, however, it reversed. We brought empty suitcases from China to the United States and bought everything there to take back to China. Complex financial relationships between the two countries affected us even on this small level.

THE UNKNOWN CHALLENGES OF A PLANNED SOCIETY

Of course, having the government so involved in planning society has its downsides. There are heavy restrictions that go so far as to dictate where people can legally live. If you want to move to a different city, you must get a government approval called a *hukou*. If you relocate without a *hukou*, your children won't be able to attend school, you'll get limited healthcare, and you will be denied certain government benefits.

In certain cities, you will see rows and rows of residential housing towers, completely empty. They are kept empty because the government has planned it out and needs to approve a certain number of people to live there. In most cases, they have used shadow banking to ensure they reach their GDP targets. It's a strange landscape where people are moved around like chess pieces. Housing vacancy rates are unclear. Some say the rate is as high as 22 percent. US rates are half that.

It's also one that is yielding big results. Today, you see companies like Huawei, ZTE, Alibaba, Tencent, and Baidu, and firms like Lenovo. The real test for these companies has been global expansion and, more importantly, positive brand recognition. Many are already on their way. Huawei leads the world in smartphones sold and in telecommunication hardware. Alibaba and Tencent continue to expand through emerging markets and venture-backed tech portfolios. They are thriving in emergent markets, partly due to the "flexible" nature of their laws and partly due to their ability to offer new solutions in areas with no legacy products. In mature markets, however, the perception of these companies remains questionable, which makes competition that much harder.

Sure, in a planned economy, you can get stuff done very efficiently and quickly, but there is still a perception that in a free economy you have more creativity and the security of a system of checks and balances. As people move into different classes and the middle class gets wider, we will see if they survive or if they change their models. The government has seemingly made a deal with the people: follow these rules and don't cause any problems, and you can continue to make money for yourself and your family. Ninety percent of the time when you ask someone in China if they'd prefer freedom or prosperity, they answer freedom.

MAJOR TAKEAWAYS

Growing up, I was taught that the free-market capitalist model employed by the US and most of the developed world was the only way. What I came to realize is that societies and countries do things differently yet successfully, and there is more than one way of doing things. What works in developed countries may not work in emerging ones.

POLITICAL SYSTEMS CAN DRIVE CREATIVITY

Something that became very clear to me in China was just how much a political system can drive creativity. There are upsides and downsides to this.

In India, they have a similar population to China, and slightly more provinces, but they lack the cohesion that comes from dictated policy. The challenge in India is a different one: how do they bring all these people together to be successful in the world's largest democracy? They will get there one day, and it will be a great accomplishment. Think of where India would be if the Brits hadn't drained all their money!

In Japan, while they plan things out, the government doesn't control private companies as tightly. In the sixties and seventies, the state controlled most of the large companies, and this lead to hyper growth, then to what is known as the "lost decades."

These different approaches yield unique results, processes, and creativity.

ADOPT A STARTUP MENTALITY

Many people in the US are afraid of looking bad and making missteps, so they tend to err on the side of being too conservative and risk-averse. While we are the home of the startup, the US startup scene has been blind to the foreign ideas and innovation that could potentially propel them even further. The arrogance in Silicon Valley through the VC and PE firms has led to an implosion in the US startup scene, which has ushered in a new wave of innovation, creativity, and a change in mindset. While there are still pockets of hubris, we are seeing innovation in places where futures once looked grim. As I am writing this, there are reports about China exceeding the US in VC funding for the first time. This is a good challenge for the US and good for the world as a whole. Companies, communities, and cities should be challenged to grow.

China also made it clear to businesses that even if you're not a startup, you need to develop a startup mentality. The question remains whether China will keep its commitment to small business development or continue to expand the state-owned enterprises. You need to consider how to innovate without fear of failure. You must test repeatedly and do things that seem unnatural to be successful. It's the only way to venture into the unknown and cause disruption in a market. We call this "controlled chaos" coupled with a herd mentality. Time will tell if it's good or bad for business.

ALIGN YOUR AIMS WITH YOUR HOST COUNTRY

For your company to be successful overseas, you need to be aware of government initiatives and goals, and you should try to align your own strategy with theirs. If the government is hot on automating processes related to manufacturing, e-commerce, immigration, autonomous vehicles, or clean energy, maybe there is an opening for your brand. Put another way, follow the money.

One of the next major pushes by many governments will

be toward boosting real-use artificial intelligence. Many companies will try to pivot to create successful partnerships that work toward that aim. The rule is if you don't align, you'll have a tough time.

THE POWER OF EXPERIENCE

By this same logic, adapting to the local economic and business system is indispensable to achieving success. Cultural awareness and immersion in a country helps a company to navigate foreign waters more readily. Understanding economics, geopolitical influences, and the key drivers in a country will help you better position your business by developing proper strategies and execution tactics.

In the developed world, we're used to certain systems and processes. A company should be pushing to go into emerging markets where business is conducted differently and rules are more lax and move faster. The only way to successfully do that is to have people embedded in the culture.

LOOK FOR CREATIVE EMPLOYEES

When you set out to hire more creative people, you should look at the differences of viewpoint and experience that they can bring to your team. In Asia, your US diversity quotes may not apply. I was the minority white guy.

Look toward their background for information on how they might be driven toward creativity. What did their generation experience? As with Millennials and Generation X employees in the United States, each generation of people has its own mentality and values. In China, I worked with people whose parents lived through famines, wars, and an unstable government. These people went hungry, were forced to wear uniforms, and faced heavy restrictions. Their history established their present in hunger, drive, and determination.

A person's unique experience can drive them, as can their experiences with failure. Sometimes, being allowed to fail is a boon to creativity. Overcoming objectives, adversity, and challenges can really make the difference between who might have more creative solutions versus who might not. Understanding someone's experience and story, and aligning that with your business's goals, will prove to be invaluable.

In the end, it's less about the educational degree or the color of someone's skin, and more about what they've experienced as individuals. How did they grow up? What were they taught? Do they have real-world experience? They might not have the same mindset as you, but that's okay. In fact, it's a wonderful thing.

LESSON 4

GRIT, NOT FEAR

Everyone experiences tragedy and hardship at some time in their life. Some experience more than others. Often, people respond to them by becoming laser-focused on certain goals to help them through the difficult times. The small details fall by the wayside, and it doesn't matter what you eat or wear, where you live, what you drive—all that just falls away when things in your life are changing dramatically. In some ways, that same type of drive is present all the time in many Chinese people. They have an incredible ability to simply focus and get things done despite major obstacles.

This focused drive toward common goals is even present in the language. The Chinese may call this *hun luan* (混乱), which can be translated into "chaos" or "disorderly," where fear motivates. Another phase may be *jian chi bu*

xie (坚持不懈), which means "persistent to the end" or
"never stop." This sentiment embedded in the language
relates to how the past has impacted their present. Their
past drives them to get things done no matter what happens in their lives. It boils down to the people's tenacity,
their grit.

FROM POVERTY TO LUXURY

In China, many people have stories of hardship that they
had to overcome. The past seventy-five years have not
been easy, and many Chinese people lived a completely
different style of life just decades ago. Over five hundred million people have come out of poverty and into
the middle class over the last thirty years, just under 35
percent of the population. This radical shift has had a
great impact on their drive to get things done no matter
what the obstacles.

A lot of foreign people hold the view that China is not a
capitalistic society, due to their state-controlled influences and monetary backing. Since there is a lack of
transparency, outsiders assume they know what communism looks like. The truth is that Chinese people are
extremely capitalistic. They are very aggressive when
doing business, out of necessity. The sheer amount of
competition within the country demands it. With the
adaptation to accumulating wealth, more opportunity

has opened to buy new things, travel, and give back to the family. The motivation is constant and even more pronounced than in more developed countries. America and China have mixed models of government influence and systems. Many books are written on capitalism, socialism, communism, and democracy. We will leave it to those mighty scholars to debate what works and what doesn't.

This sharp contrast between those who have risen to the middle and upper class (primarily in the cities) and those who still lead a more rustic life became clear to me during my business travels throughout the country.

During my time there, I watched the infrastructure and country develop significantly. In the early days of my tenure, the infrastructure wasn't all there, particularly in the interior of the country. Foreign business was being conducted in coastal cities like Shanghai, Beijing, and special economic zones in Shenzhen and Guangzhou. When I went on sales calls in remote cities like Tianjin or Xuzhou, which still had millions of people, traveling was an adventure.

One time on our way to Tianjin, our flight to Beijing was delayed due to "air congestion," code for military maneuvers. My colleagues and I missed our connection, and since we had to be in Tianjin, a neighboring city, by a certain time, the only way to get there was to take the bus.

Chinese intercity buses are a unique experience. I was the only white guy, in a suit, on a bus full of farmers, produce, and live animals. The bus made all kinds of noises and was beat up. It would stop at seemingly random places on the highway with no buildings in sight and let people on or off. I'd watch these people walk off into the distance across fields of snow. I had never seen anything like this before. It was eye-opening. Moreover, we made it to the city in time for our sales call! To me, it represented this drive to get things done no matter what the situation or the small inconveniences along the way.

The US is the land of convenience. Some people aren't used to working through obstacles or aren't familiar with dealing with the unknown. They don't have this all-encompassing drive to get things done no matter the situation. For the Chinese, it's the most normal thing. They'd say that the rickety bus we took was a pretty good bus because it was still better than riding a bike.

MENTALITY SHIFTS

When you talk to individuals who grew up in China, their stories and their families' stories are heroic. No matter what was going on in their lives or in the country's politics and laws, they overcame every challenge. Few people in the developed world would be able to manage these obstacles the same way. The Chinese are driven and always in for a good fight. The Chinese are driven by an almost fight-or-flight mentality.

In a country where so much of life is orderly and systematic, work schedules are all-encompassing. People work long hours, over weekends and holidays, without a second thought. In fact, they think it is necessary to work those hours to achieve their goal or give the right impression to their bosses. There are three weeks in the whole year, during Chinese New Year, the Moon Festival, and the Spring Festival, when people might take a vacation. This what some call the greatest human migration on earth, as three hundred to four hundred million people travel to see their families. Otherwise, they are working eighty- to ninety-hour weeks and at all hours of the night, a version of the Soviet worker's model. I found it hard to believe that people in developed countries would want to work that hard.

This workaholic drive has a lot to do with how China has evolved. It has evolved as a manufacturing hub and now is transitioning into one that provides services. With the growth of wealth, the types of services and products offered to the world are changing. China has seen a bit of everything, from imperialism to dictatorship and military rule, each with its own opportunities, challenges, and risks. But that initial robotic worker mentality still resides in many people who have moved to white-collar professions. Part of the mindset that helped get so many people out of poverty and into the middle class is an individual drive to win at all costs and a patience for taking the long view. The one-party system will continue to require a force to serve as a check and balance to plans and decisions that could impact generations. Maybe the world stage will serve as that check, with continued pressure to change and reform.

Their tough origin stories also contribute to a lack of fear of failure. Many of the people I interacted with were open-minded and amenable to change. They were continually involved in the learning process, asking questions and always trying to understand more. If they failed at something, it simply made them more motivated to move in the direction of success.

It was rare that any of my colleagues told me that something couldn't be done. On the unusual occasion when someone did say they couldn't do something, it really meant that there was an underlying problem, whether related to corruption, business laws, or government initiatives that put roadblocks in place. This prompted the necessity to ask questions. Living and doing business in China makes you learn to ask questions and get to the bottom of what drives certain behaviors and actions.

The Western business tradition is historically more

risk-averse, whether entering a new market or testing a new service or product. There's always hesitancy and an underlying fear of failure. I didn't feel that with my Chinese counterparts, especially when they were developing or figuring out solutions. There was always a way to get things done. It was a refreshing mentality.

MAJOR TAKEAWAYS

Experiencing the characteristics of the Chinese mentality and drive really changed my mindset and my tolerance for being uncomfortable.

GET COMFORTABLE BEING UNCOMFORTABLE

It made me value the experience of being uncomfortable. It also made me accept more easily that I would experience failures as well as success. If you're not uncomfortable while doing it, it probably means you're not stretching far enough. When you get too comfortable, it's probably time to change.

Unknowns, risks, and problems are things that you should learn to value when doing business in China. There will be times when you're not going to understand. There will be many routes you can take. You're going to fail, and you're going to learn from it.

BUILD YOUR BUSINESS LIKE A RAILROAD

In the US, we talk about rebuilding infrastructure and bridges that are collapsing, and the $2 trillion needed to repair existing infrastructure. In direct contrast, because of China's initiatives and ability to dictate, they're able to execute plans very quickly. At one point in time, China was building one hundred new airports simultaneously across the whole country. This type of environment and pace of developing infrastructure is foreign to us. In the US, bureaucracy gets in the way of any rapid change. It undermines our priorities and what matters in the long run. On the other hand, you could question the large debt loads for infrastructure and if government lending to itself is sustainable.

There are more rail lines in China than in any other country in the world. They stretch over twenty-five thousand kilometers. People can now go practically anywhere in the country by high-speed rail. To go from Shanghai to Beijing, almost eleven hundred kilometers, now takes two and a half hours. Furthermore, these rail lines were developed and built in relatively no time at all.

Compare that to India, which built one single rail line out of Bangalore and started the project in the late 1990s. There, bureaucracy and corruption delayed it for almost twenty years. India is no different from China in terms of population and people. It's just the system of government that makes the big difference. China had plans in place and executed them with extreme precision and drive. This mentality bleeds into the people and drives them to get things done.

Having people like this in your organization speeds up the process of developing the kind of mindset and attitude that companies need. It's important to seek out such people who have an international mindset. Recruit them and hire them into the right positions. The drive and attitude to get things done then becomes contagious. It's invaluable for these people to be involved in leadership and the strategic growth of a company.

Of the many things that widened my perspective, one of them was the way my Chinese colleagues were completely unafraid of big numbers. There are so many people and so much opportunity that the people are naturally unafraid to scale to certain numbers. Population levels of 1.4 billion are hard to comprehend when measured against the US's 370 million or so. Think big, do big!

When I returned to the US, the scope of business I was doing seemed small. It all seemed easier because of this. It changed my whole mindset. It fueled my creativity and my drive to be more efficient. In fact, it motivated me to start a business from the ground up. I quit Dell and ventured into the world of startups. I don't think I would have done so had I not experienced a shift in mindset during my time in China.

SHARE YOUR GRIT BACK HOME

People who have worked abroad often have more experience with the sort of all-encompassing hard work needed to meet near-impossible goals. They are often used to surprises, obstacles, and challenges. They can offer a different viewpoint on products and services. If you have experience seeing what can be accomplished in other places, it feeds your determination and motivation to replicate it for your own company.

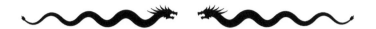

BE HUMBLE...OR BE HUMBLED

When I led my first sales team in China, I had trouble getting my employees to conform to the behavior I expected. I wanted my team to adopt a standard Western process of putting sales leads and information into a spreadsheet we called a funnel. This was a new process to them, and they wouldn't update the charts properly, often making mistakes or, worse, entering fictitious deals and inflated sales opportunities. Many of my team members only spoke broken English. Even if they didn't understand what I said, they would nod their heads to save face.

After about six months of slow progress, I began to get frustrated reviewing and rereviewing the same deals. I would speak more loudly and more aggressively, something typical in America but extremely out of place in a Chinese office space. I could not understand why people were not motivated to get this done.

I couldn't seem to impress on them how vital this was to the success of our company. If we didn't do it, we would all be in the poor house. At one point, I remember saying, "If we don't do this, we're all going to be riding bikes to work!"

Right after I said that, I realized that some of them probably did ride their bikes to work. The infrastructure wasn't set up for anything else, and there were millions of bikes on the road. My closed-minded view was that everyone drove cars, lived in homes, and basically had the same sort of middle-class lifestyle I was used to. I had inadvertently insulted them.

This was a serious reminder to me that to get things done, I needed to adopt different tactics than I was used to. I couldn't just walk in with a "we know best" perspective and tell everyone what they were doing was wrong, according to me. I had been humbled, and it colored the rest of my time there. In Chinese, they may call this *qian xu* (谦虚), which means "humble."

SHIFTING MANAGEMENT STYLE

Prior to China, I had only managed people in the United States who were mostly from the same culture as I was. Managing people in a foreign country was a new experience for me, and I struggled to form connections with my new employees. Trying to motivate them was even harder.

It took me a long time to understand how to properly motivate people in a different country. My management style had to change, and it did dramatically over those ten years. I used to be more aggressive. I'd tell people they had to hit a certain goal, and I didn't care how they got there. In China and Japan, employees would simply nod and agree, even if they didn't understand what you wanted them to do. I'd be waiting and waiting to get a plan back from my people, and it would never come. They'd say they were still working on it even if they didn't know how to even begin.

My own tendency not to ask a lot of questions only contributed to this. I wasn't looking to understand how they got things done or who they were as individuals. As a result, they didn't offer to help and let me flounder. In those early days, I lost a lot of people, and the business suffered.

I started to take a more prescriptive approach, walking

people through the five or ten steps required to do a task. It was a shift from "Do this" to "Why don't you try this?" Whereas before I could set people loose without really caring or understanding how they got things done, I now had to pay more attention. I would ask myself, "Why am I asking them to do this? How can I word this differently? What's my end game?" I had to think through the whole process to manage effectively.

Another thing that contributed to our communication issues was that most foreign leaders only stayed on-site for one or two years before returning home. As a result, some local employees would simply wait out a manager they didn't gel with. They knew that if they waited long enough, another person would come in and completely change things around again. If they didn't like you, they could wait you out.

PARADIGM SHIFTS

I once worked with a Singaporean coworker to plan my organization in terms of people and business. It was early on in my career, so I thought I knew everything. She had been in China for a while and obviously knew more than I did. I asked her why people weren't taking the initiative to get the results we needed. I couldn't understand why we weren't first out of the gate, making the kind of progress I wanted.

She looked at me and said, "Well, you know in the US, the saying is that the early bird gets the worm. In China, it's the early bird gets their head chopped off."

It took a second for that to sink in. Part of my employees' culture and upbringing discouraged them from taking charge and leading the pack. It humbled me again and made me change my style. I went from wondering why they didn't look for more creative solutions and operate outside the rules to asking myself, "How do I pull my employees out of their comfort zones and set a good example? How can I be more prescriptive so they can be more efficient? How can I learn more about what motivates them?"

My prescriptive guidance made me think more about what I was saying and how I was communicating. The longer I spent abroad, the more I felt my English becoming simplified and more efficient. When I returned to the US, I was using fewer complex words because I was emphasizing communication fit.

COMPANIES ON THE INSIDE TRACK

When you looked at the personal computer space in 2004 and 2005, most PCs sold inside the US market were made by US companies. The space was dominated by companies like IBM, HP, Dell, and Compaq, with only smaller contributions from a couple of Japanese companies like Sony and Toshiba.

Local companies dominate local markets. Big American companies like IBM and Dell didn't even rank second or third. People wanted to buy local, they were familiar with local companies, and the local economy was slated to give local companies a boost over foreign ones.

In China, the law explicitly favors domestic companies. In order to sell your wares, companies need the proper certification and paperwork. Local companies like Lenovo may receive information about these requirements long before foreign companies get to find out. If computers were now required to feature a certain kind of certification, then local companies were given a head start to get their engineers working on development.

Some companies that had connections in the government would prewire their approvals so that everything was in line and ready to go as soon as the regulatory announcements were made. When it came to foreign companies, they would receive less notice to change all their processes and get approvals.

Because of these imbalances, foreign companies would lose business. Lenovo would get bigger contracts with individuals or stall competition growth. There was no legal recourse to take because, while the legal system exists, it hardly enforces anything.

As a result, foreign companies in China were constantly forced into a reactive stance. Companies that were extremely powerful industry titans at home were forcibly humbled and shaped by China's rules and laws. A good example is the introduction of data-intensive companies like banks and internet-based businesses. The government requires foreign companies doing business in China to store their data locally inside the country's borders. This forced companies to build and manage this server infrastructure locally. Today's battles are all about data, how you get it, who has access to it, and who can share it.

SAVING FACE

One thing I had never experienced before were letters of apology to business leaders for mistakes made. This is very prevalent in Asia. A lot of things can go wrong when running a business inside a foreign country. For example, when we had issues in China with our laptops overheating, one province required us to submit a formal letter to them describing the issue, what our resolution was, how sorry we were that it had happened, and our commitment that it wouldn't happen again. At first, this seemed silly to me. Later, I realized that these letters made it easier for my superiors to report incidents back to their superiors.

It happened in Japan as well, but this time for missing shipping deadlines. We had logistics issues, and a company we worked with needed equipment by certain times to run their business. Since we missed delivery times, their business couldn't run. At first, when I was told we needed to send them an apology letter, I blew it off. I thought it wasn't a big deal. It wasn't until we lost that business that I realized we had to conform and adapt.

It took a little while, but once I understood the process, I could relay it back to headquarters and teach them how to do it on their own. Conforming in these areas was a way of building relationships and trust even when things were not going well.

BLUNDERING

Even today, I still catch myself making cultural blunders. I am much more aware of them these days, but it still happens. Blundering can be light, for example, calling an Aussie a Kiwi. They may not like it very much, but it can be joked about. In other cases, it can be a much more sensitive topic like confusing Hong Kong with mainland China. In this case, referring to someone by the improper identity would be a huge blunder because there is a lot of animosity between the areas.

To mainland Chinese, people from Hong Kong fled during

the cultural revolution and separated themselves from China. On the other hand, Hong Kong people tend to see themselves as superior to mainland Chinese. I remember once even seeing the *South China Morning Post* refer to the mainland Chinese as roaches. This was in a newspaper! This same intense animosity applies to Taiwanese and mainland Chinese and even with Malaysian Chinese and mainland Chinese.

I made a lot of mistakes about where people were from. I learned early on to ask the question "Where are you from?" even when it seemed obvious. Years later, it became easier to tell by someone's last name, appearance, and how they spoke. For example, the difference between Cantonese and Mandarin is pretty easy to spot, as is Singaporean English. On the other hand, there is always room for error with such a vast geography, history, and a country with over 1,300 dialects. Some of the only constants are the written characters.

Some jokes that are appropriate in the West don't fly well in the East, and sarcasm is one of them. In the US and the West, sarcasm is more commonplace. At first, I was constantly confusing people and quickly learned that sarcasm didn't work well in speeches or when talking to an audience. Part of my management technique in the US was saying funny things and getting people to laugh, but that had to change. The East has a different mentality and sense of humor. To be funny, you need an understanding of the people, politics, and current events. I needed to adapt.

MAJOR TAKEAWAYS

There are always multiple ways to get things done. The way you grew up and what you bring to the table is valuable, but it's just one way out of many. Other countries have different complexities and may seem to turn right when you turn left and turn left when you turn right. In foreign cultures, it's important to be aware, understanding, and open to learn, even through mistakes.

THE HUMBLE SURVIVE

The faster companies adopt humility, openness, and different mindsets, the better the companies will fare. This applies most to businesses here in the US looking to expand outside of mature markets. A humble attitude is the only way to build trust with your global counterparts.

ADAPT YOUR MANAGEMENT STYLE

With humility must come the ability to be flexible with your management style. Adapting to a local mindset and being culturally aware of each person's unique mindset will affect how you manage them. It doesn't mean you should disregard your company's best practices, but it does mean learning from other cultures and being multi-directional when approaching best practices. A lot of the best practices I've adopted have come from other parts of the world. Being open to change will only help develop your management style.

BEND TO THE GOVERNMENT

Finally, humility in the face of a different system of government is significant. Certain governments have more influence on business than others. In China, government initiatives drive almost everything. It's important to understand those initiatives and analyze how they figure into your business model. The more you understand what the government wants, the more likely you'll be aligned with the right businesses and the right people.

In the US, there is a lot of lobbying and spending to influence political figures (some might call this a legal form of bribery), but you can't necessarily do that in China. They already have a ten-year plan with initiatives flowing out of that plan. You could also say there is a hundred-year plan to establish China back on the world stage. For example, China is focusing on better healthcare, automation via AI, technology to help people live, and eradication of poverty by 2020. Aligning your business with these initiatives is a wise decision.

ALIGNING PERSPECTIVES

Just like you have your perceptions of your peers, colleagues, and foreign counterparts, they have certain perceptions of you too. You could talk to various people across the globe about their perceptions of Americans, and you'd get different answers from all of them, as well as some similarities. In China and Japan, they think everybody in Texas is a rancher or cowboy, wearing a hat and boots. These perceptions can help you build your relationships with others. As you learn about someone else's culture, they can learn about yours. It allows both of you to be humbled and connect better with each other and the truth.

I have friends from all over the world, as do my kids. Our mutual perceptions of each other have changed and allowed us to better understand one another. This has made me a better leader. It also helps me remember that I am going to make mistakes.

There are going to be problems. You'll fall on your face once or twice and end up in a bad situation. All of that is okay. If you accept these mistakes and turn them into advantages, you can grow as an individual. It will serve you in the future at other jobs, roles, and companies. It's all in the practice of being humbled, and it's always a learning process.

ADAPTABILITY IS EVERYTHING

When you walk into a foreign market with a diverse team, you must be adaptable. You may go overboard to push a certain thing, and your employees will bend over backwards to please you, but it won't happen every time. You may only be able to change a few things here or there. In the long run, you have to figure out how to acclimate your processes to their environment, which takes time. It requires asking questions and adopting a local mindset.

I've seen it in my own experience and among other Western businesspeople trying to force their way into a foreign setting. It always seems to fail or yield less-than-impressive results. What it takes to achieve in a foreign environment is to recognize that you're not in control. Usually, this idea makes people uncomfortable. In the US, you work at company, you learn a process, and you do it. It becomes part of your subconscious, and you gain this feeling of control. That feeling dissipates in foreign markets.

Once you are humbled by these different dynamics, you're able to adopt a different stance or look at it a different way. You learn to ask more questions and connect more easily with others.

LESSON 6

ACCEPTANCE

In my early years in China, I used to have to fly to Beijing weekly to meet with sales teams. My days were very busy, and I'd hardly have time to eat. As a result, I usually scarfed down whatever food they deigned to serve on the plane.

On one flight, I happened to sit next to another foreigner. We were cordial and didn't say much, but he watched me scarf down my airplane meal, which was some unidentifiable pork dish. Close to landing, we started chatting. He asked me if I liked the pork, and I told him I was starving and would have eaten anything they gave me.

"I don't do that anymore," he told me. "You know how pork works here in China?"

I had no idea. I wasn't paying attention to that sort of thing. I just assumed China had regulations akin to the FDA and everything was processed appropriately. I was wrong. The man pointed out the window to these giant mountains of trash we were flying over. "You see that trash? It's imported from all over the world. You know what's running all over it?" I looked out the window and could see groups of animals around the trash piles. He continued, "Those are pigs. They feed the pigs the garbage because pigs will eat anything."

There were miles of pigs, millions of them, lined up eating the garbage. My stomach turned. As you might expect, I stopped eating pork after that. It wasn't easy because pork is incredibly prevalent in China. In fact, the United States imports a good chunk of its pork from China as well, and up until 2018, we exported a good amount of our garbage to China. So that's something to think about.

It was just one of the many facts of life in a foreign country that I had to learn to accept and embrace.

MAINTAINING EQUILIBRIUM

When you move to a foreign country, you will inevitably encounter new experiences that you could not expect or plan for. In China, these unexpected factors included squat toilets, smog, TB and other illnesses (my son contracted bird flu), family stress, safety concerns, and a complete lack of understanding from friends and family back home.

These sorts of culture shocks all change you on a very basic level. The Chinese may call this *zhen* (震), which means "dealing with shocking events," or *zhen han* (震撼), which means "a strong emotional impact on people, a release of energy that results in shocking events." To me, these reactions go something like this: hubris, shock and denial, a feeling of knowing nothing, wanting to start over, and finally, a humbled sense of balance. Unfortunately, it's not a linear process. You bounce back and forth among the stages before you finally achieve equilibrium.

The advice of the sages is that it's important to stay internally centered even when the world around you is tilting on its axis. We must learn to accept unexpected and unpredictable events as a part of life and, in the process, change ourselves to maintain equilibrium and prosper in our environment.

I had to roll with many strange and unexpected events during one bizarre weekend trip in China. During my second year, I decided to incentivize one of my sales teams by offering them a trip if we reached a certain goal. I let them decide on a place, and they chose a location up near the North Korean border. I wasn't too keen on going there, but they hit their goal, so we planned our weekend trip up north.

That Friday, we flew into the tiny Yanji (Yanbian) airport in Jilin province and took a bus to a hotel right on the border. It was an adventure. The Chinese side was lit up and full of activity, while the North Korean side was pitch black. There were a lot of churches on the border, and it seemed to be a refuge for those fleeing North Korea. Signs with Korean characters were everywhere, and it almost felt like being there. Every time we made a stop, the locals all wanted pictures with "the white guy."

The next morning, our first trip was a car ride up Mount Changhai (the Koreans call it Mount Paektu) to a frozen volcanic crater that the Chinese call Heaven Lake. For the ethnic Manchus, this was a sacred ancestral site. For the Koreans, it was the alleged birthplace of Kim Jung Il.

On the bus back down the mountain, we stopped at a sort of zoo. There were large crowds of people clustered around to see large animals, and they claimed to have twenty tigers. I could also see a price board with pictures of chickens, goats, and cows. I wasn't sure what to make of that, but later, I came across a small chain-link cage filled with roosters next to a cage full of bears. A huge crowd had gathered around to look at the bears. Suddenly, a guy holding a live rooster by the legs threw it into the bear cage. The bear immediately started mauling the rooster. I was shocked, but the crowd loved it.

Noticing my shock, one of my Chinese colleagues asked me if we had this type of thing in the US. No, definitely not, I told him. This would not fly there. He looked confused, as if to ask, "Why not?" The entire experience reminded me of how closed off culturally our two sides of the world were from each other.

Later, my team asked me if I wanted to go see the Bengal tigers. The park workers loaded twenty-five people into a short bus meant for eighteen with bars over the windows. We drove past a gate, and the entire time I was thinking, "Oh my god, what am I getting into?" After we entered the tiger park, these huge tigers began coming toward the bus. They were very aggressive and looked as if they hadn't eaten. I just sat there with wide eyes in utter disbelief. My colleagues were unaffected by the experience; it was completely normal to them. It was all so strange to me. I didn't know if I was safe or if the bus would break down, leaving us stranded with a pack of hungry tigers. None of it was up to the standards I was used to. After that ride, I'd seen enough.

Or so I thought. Upon leaving the front gate of the park, a woman started speaking loudly to our group, on and on. It turned out that on Saturdays, there was a free tiger-feeding show. At first, I was reticent, but then I thought, "When will I ever get a chance like that again?" So we headed back into the park.

We waited for the 4:00 p.m. showing outside a large circle surrounded by a chain-link fence. At around 4:25 p.m., we heard a cow moaning loudly. One man was pulling it by a rope, and another was pushing it from behind into the circle. The tigers had been pacing inside a second adjoining fenced area. The tiger gate opened, and the tiger rushed the cow, jumping on it, attacking its legs. I still remember its deafening squeals. The crowd went nuts.

That weekend stayed with me for a long time. It was a unique experience, even though it was shocking. It also made me think that I knew nothing about the world. In the end, I just had to accept that things are different there. It's futile to go into a foreign country and expect the people to share your sensibilities. You don't live in America anymore. It's not your rules and norms. The only way that you can be effective at getting things done is by accepting the country as it is.

FLEXIBLE LAWS

In China, there are always multiple interpretations of laws, depending on the current times. There is a flexibility in how things are done, which typically favors one side and could be called unfair by outsiders. The Chinese may call this *ling huo* (灵活), or "doing things flexibly." Just like the United States, China has a system of laws based on morality; however, unlike the US, these laws are often creatively interpreted or not applied at all. It goes along with the Chinese concept of *yin and yang*, a constant need for harmony and a balance between good and bad, or opposite forces that are complementary. The laws are more flexible depending on whose needs they serve.

Take, for example, China's intense traffic situation. Most traffic laws are outright ignored, making the streets look like a complicated ballet of anarchy. People on bikes and mopeds get hit all the time. You would see them lying in the street, and nobody would stop and offer to help them. Only foreigners would sometimes venture to lend a hand. The reason for this neglect is that if a bystander helps, they may find themselves tied to the problem. They might be sued by the victim for providing improper help. If there has been a crime, they might find themselves implicated despite their good intentions.

If there is a car accident, the two drivers usually try to work out compensation right there on the spot. Someone pays someone off instead of taking the issue to court. Police may come, but they usually just help with negotiations of the settlement.

I was also told that if a foreigner was in a car that got into an accident, the best course of action was to leave the scene and the car. Most people assume that foreigners have money, so they try to extort it from them.

This has changed recently with the implementation of AI technology in surveillance cameras. Facial recognition and social credit systems are keeping people more in line, which questions the overall purpose of CCTV and technology.

For better or worse, that's how the Chinese think and how their society works. It may be the result of extreme competition in a society so large and still growing. But it's a constant. If there's a public dispute or a fight breaks out, crowds will gather, and nobody does anything about it. Compare this to the US and the rest of the developed world, where it's frowned upon to not do something. The Chinese don't want to get involved with issues related to the law.

BUSINESS IMPLICATIONS

Lack of regulation or adherence to the rules has an impact on business practices as well.

In the US, we have regulations and agencies that provide credit ratings for companies and debt. It isn't a perfect system, but it works okay. In China, the financial credit system is very much missing. Not too long ago, you had to pay cash for everything. Thanks to a surge in technology, transactions are mostly electronic now, but early on, credit was not given to local companies by foreign businesses. For a company to do business with another company, they needed a bank guarantee, meaning the bank had to provide them with a letter stating that they have cash or a receipt that they could take as payment.

Foreign companies doing business in China had problems all the time with collecting money. It buried some companies and dented their plans for quick expansion. Internal checks and balances, having the right people with the right connections in collection roles, and due diligence prior to selling, all lead to manageable transactions. Government and personal relationships played key roles in the balance of business. In the US, we have trade credit: net 30, net 60, and net 90. There's recourse of some kind if it's not paid, and collection agencies begin to hound the borrowers. The lack of this in China led to a lot of bad business transactions.

Foreign companies would come in all the time eager to do business and jump on big opportunities and sales. They'd build the product, ship it out, and then never get paid. They'd argue and argue, but there was no legal recourse for them to get their money back. The government wouldn't want to get involved.

It happened all too often, and a lot of companies and subsidiaries went out of business or decided to leave. In my company, we found a way to work around that. We could build orders, accept orders, and do any kind of business, but we always required the money up front.

I'm sure this is less common now, and will be less so the further along China progresses, but it's a big issue that the country must address. These days, there's talk, and some action, about social credit systems. It's yet to be determined how this would work with limited checks and balances by the government, but it's a starting point to oversight of business and institutions. Again, the larger issue is the opening of the financial system, convertible currency, and overall transparency.

On another side of the spectrum, at my organization, we had a lot of weekly transactions that happened on the last day of the week. Seventy-five to 80 percent of our business was done on Fridays because many of these companies couldn't secure cash or didn't have cash in the bank until then, or they were still trying to negotiate terms, price, channel partners, etc. It's all about who blinks first! A lot of competing companies in other provinces would land a bid based on who could get their money in the bank first.

In China, there was a lot of fake currency floating around,

just like there are fake goods and products, and even factories that make fake products. Tellers would test for fake currency. If a bill stood out, they would point it out to you and give it right back instead of confiscating it. Nobody calls the police, as would be the case back in America. In the US, fake currency on that scale would be a major scandal.

My assumption is that most of this type of fraud has decreased or isn't as prevalent now. Mobile payments have resolved many of these issues. It may be pushed deeper into the underworld or into other emerging countries where China is building economic ties.

IT'S COMPLICATED

In China and a few other places in Asia, there's a tendency to use the phrase "It's complicated" to explain things away. In my Western view, if something is complicated, you work it through. You do so by asking questions and trying to solve the problem. In the beginning, I found it frustrating to not get further details from people.

Later, I realized the true meaning of the phrase and its connotations. "It's complicated" meant that there were other personal interests involved or potentially some kind of corruption or illegal activity. It meant "We shouldn't be talking about this." From then on, it stuck in my mind that, frequently, there are conditions at play in the background that you are not privy to and may never fully know about.

As I built up trust with my employees and started asking more questions, I began to better understand the "complications." I knew someone was getting paid and why. In some cases, I had to remove some team members who were too heavily involved in some sort of complicated activity or avoid them all together. I would have completely missed these issues earlier on in my time there, and I still probably only grasped a small percentage of what was going on.

I find it quite funny these days when a foreigner on TV who is conducting business with the Chinese or another Asian country says the words "It's complicated." People often only focus on surface problems and have limited knowledge of the interworkings cross-culturally.

SHADY BUSINESS PRACTICES

When the internet was taking hold in China, many of the foreign companies located there adopted online bidding activities. Sometimes our internet would cut off during the bidding process because we were winning or we were getting more than our share. Third parties were being maneuvered to facilitate the success of one company. Shady activities like this would happen all the time. We would just scratch our heads and say, "This is crazy," but it wasn't, not in China. We had no recourse. There were people who would listen but not take any action to change the results.

Competitors would send people to go work for their rivals as double agents. There were more than likely taps into phone calls. We were very aware of the potential for espionage, and we had to be guarded about any information we shared. For example, we once let "slip" to a group of employees that we were bidding one price up front for a project, but when the time came, we lowered the bid. We ended up winning that bid and probably not without some two-faced employee inadvertently helping us out. With time and trust-building, we learned how to find the employees we could confide in.

WHEN THE SHADY GETS MALICIOUS

Extreme cases of corruption involve physical harm or even kidnapping. I have witnessed both. In some cases, foreigners brought in to "clean up" businesses require their own security detail due to safety risks. In other cases, people just disappear for long periods of time, and you may or may not see them again.

Business can be so cutthroat that kidnappings are not unheard of. Influential company players risk being kidnapped by rival companies, held for either ransom or influence.

To some, this may sound unbelievable. For others, it's a way of life. Until you are exposed to activities of this nature, you may sit in a cloud of ignorant bliss. They happen and will continue to happen. It opens your eyes to a world that is not governed by law but by old tactics of fear and heavy-handedness. Many of these situations have to be fixed by individuals who have "friends" in the right places and connections (*guanxi*).

This is a glaring example of the criminal underbelly that is very much present in China. A lot of stuff happens through personal connections. If you aren't aware of who someone is and how they're connected, you can potentially miss big things. At Dell, instead of fighting it completely, we tried to regulate it. We tried to project our American business values onto China's business values in an attempt to control issues by toeing the line. The truth is that you can never really control it all. You can only try to regulate it as much as you can.

MAJOR TAKEAWAYS

In a foreign country, going against the grain often just makes things harder for you. The more quickly you accept the way things are, the more quickly you can move on to solving problems and understanding specific business practices.

ACCEPT AND ADAPT

Most people want to learn more. Most people want to change, but they have a tough time making those changes because they aren't completely aware. It's like with kids who say they can't do something new, even though they've never tried. Yet taking on new challenges is how we grow. Sometimes you succeed and sometimes you fail, but you always grow in the process. As we grow in our experiences, we learn to accept more, and our view of the world expands with that acceptance.

EVALUATING RISK

If you accept the business practices in another country, you need to also be aware of the risks. If you don't know about the risks, you need to ask a lot of questions.

Many business practices have a level of risk. You might want to stay away from those at the top end, but staying in the middle area and helping things go with the flow can certainly help you. A lot of Chinese words are related to this need for harmony. They live in a world that is changing. It's a world with a different mindset than our Western one. To work in that world requires learning how to find balance and harmony. This is part of acceptance.

DEALING WITH UNETHICAL BUSINESS PRACTICES

Bribery and underhanded dealings are a fact of life in many countries across the world. No matter how much you disapprove, the reality is that sometimes there will be bribes occurring around your business. Early on, I wasn't aware of how commonplace it was. In fact, I was shocked that it was happening so freely.

From a moral standpoint, I didn't agree with bribing people. As time went on, I became increasingly aware of when it was happening, and I tried to avoid putting my company in those positions.

It's also important to be cognizant of the Foreign Corrupt Practices Act (FCPA). All US companies and their employees can be held liable for any actions not in line with US laws and regulations. This includes bribery and doing business with banned nations.

What we find objectionable is more commonplace in other cultures. You're never going to come out 100 percent pure. That sentiment is part of the Chinese mentality and the world they grow up in. Sometimes you must work through third parties to get something done. It's how business has been conducted there for thousands of years, so why should it change? Who's to say we're right and they're wrong?

In mature markets, when things go bad, people talk to their government representatives. The Chinese don't air dirty laundry in public. That's their mindset. Part of acceptance is doing things the way they're done in a country versus what you're used to. You will be confronted with unethical practices. You may even be asked to provide bribes of some kind. Sometimes there are workarounds. Other times, you must just walk away.

Part of working around these ethical gray areas is to be able to put policies and penalties in place that will help curb issues but not try to solve them. You need to try and protect your business and the individuals in it, but you should accept that you're in a world where shady activities do happen.

EMERGING MARKETS ARE CUTTHROAT

Emerging markets are cutthroat. Competition is fierce, and people have no problem putting other companies out of business. If you fall behind, don't expect help. You can turn competition and urgency in emerging markets into a good thing. You just should be willing to move at a higher speed and take the speed bumps.

After China, no challenge in the US seemed insurmountable. Most people I know here have never known anyone who got kidnapped or had to fire people for taking bribes. Being exposed to difference and challenges taught me more about what's important, what matters, and who matters. It forced me to get out of my comfort zone and to learn new things.

To fully understand and transition into new situations, you need to establish a level of trust between yourself and your employees. If people see you faltering personally or professionally and they don't know you very well, they will offer a very limited amount of help. If you falter and show weakness, you may find that your support evaporates. As time goes on and you build trust and connections with people, the amount of help you'll receive grows. It takes time and patience.

China continues to develop. It has built enormous infrastructure. There are new cities with all new planes, trains, and automobiles. It's dirty and polluted. There is crime. There is also enormous opportunity and endless drive. There are positives and negatives, but bad stuff is going to happen to you or your business. You can't let that stop you from going where business resides worldwide.

LESSON 7

PATIENCE

I always tell people that the number one skill I learned during my time in China was how to be patient. Some people think patience is an innate trait that you either have or don't, but it's really a skill you can cultivate over time. When you're working abroad, it's also a necessary coping mechanism for not driving yourself crazy.

During my work, I often attended business meetings that involved trilingual translation. I would speak in English, which would then be translated into Japanese for some of the individuals and then translated again into Chinese. The Chinese person would respond, it would be translated into Japanese, and then finally I would hear their answer in English. I always wondered how much information was lost in this convoluted game of linguistics. Literally lost in translation.

Interactions like this take a lot of time. Not only do you need to slow down your own words, you must patiently wait for the translations and then deliver the correct response. While conducting a meeting in English might only take half an hour, doing the same business with multiple languages could take three times that.

You must simplify your words in these transactions. English is riddled with slang and idioms that might be difficult to translate or lead to requests for clarification. Then, you must be patient to understand the other person and then say the right things back. Chinese, likewise, is full of idioms and sayings that can often translate oddly.

Eventually, you pick up more of a foreign language, the numbers, and slang, and you can grab hold of the context of meetings more readily. I found that staying quiet and using the few words you know in the language will allow people to drop their barriers and be more real with you.

No matter how careful you are, there will inevitably be misunderstandings, and it's your job to clarify and make sure that you are understood. Part of patience is constantly reminding yourself who you're talking to, why this meeting matters, what various actions mean in this specific cultural context, and how the different players are motivated. In fact, I find it useful to use a translator for this specific reason. It slows me down and allows me time to think more effectively.

PATIENCE AS A CULTURAL TRAIT

The Chinese culture has been around for five thousand years, and for many of those years, not a lot changed. People farmed, they fought, and they had different clans. With the evolution of technology and foreign influence, things started to speed up in the eighties, but their philosophy stayed the same.

In China, people are more patient, persistent, determined, and dedicated to long-term goals. They aren't seeking immediate gratification like Americans often are, but they do have an enormous appetite for money and success. In the US, we always want to do things fast and move on.

The Chinese have several different expressions that represent the concept of work patience. *Ren* (忍) means "the patience of the job." It refers to the Chinese tendency to tackle tasks with carefully thought out precision that often comes from long and slow deliberation and contemplation. Impatience and rash actions are viewed as irresponsible and reckless. In short: the Chinese do not like to be rushed. The Chinese penchant for orderliness effects all aspects of life and society. Everything is organized in a traditional manner, from social campaigns down to interpersonal relationships. This rigidity means that everyone and everything must wait its proper turn.

It's not that the Chinese have no sense of urgency. They just measure themselves carefully. If something is on a list of business goals or country goals, it's certain to get done quite quickly once given the green light. Without that green light, they are very patient and can wait things out until the time is right.

China is well known for the government's unique social and economic plans. Their planning is unlike anything elsewhere in the world. Some of their plans are systemic and influenced by their Soviet-era influence and the one-party system. Some of the strategic development of their economy comes from things they've picked up from neighboring countries like South Korea and Japan. In all cases, their planning cycles are very effective. Yes, there are downsides, but they tend to really accomplish the initiatives they set and pursue.

Both the government and individuals participate in these planning cycles. They're dictated on a policy level and then driven down. Think about how long it takes to drive healthcare reform in the US. The US system is more complex, has too many layers, and is grossly inefficient. China's policies aren't as impeded by bureaucracy. They are forward-looking and longer term. They also actively use feedback from key leaders in different provinces to assess what worked and what didn't in their experimental models. It's the reason they've grown so much and so fast in the last thirty years.

Five years ago, there were over five hundred experiments happening concurrently in different provinces and cities across the country. They were testing new ways of doing healthcare, implementing AI-based technology, and managing cities through smart technology. It allowed them to create a feedback loop and make changes. It's very much an engineering mentality (in fact, many past and current leaders have engineering backgrounds and have been educated in US universities), the same way businesses work to drive innovation and strategically move in a certain direction.

LONG-TERM VERSUS SHORT-TERM MINDSET

Sometimes being patient means playing the long game. I've taken many deals that looked bad on paper but were, in fact, gateways to success farther down the road. I've negotiated opportunities with customers in China that I would never have allowed in a more mature market. Whether it was huge discounts, free services, or something attached to the product itself, it meant finding a creative way to have a beachhead into a customer. Some of these deals were just handshakes or by trust, things I would only do there.

These were viewed as acts of good faith on the part of the customers because they knew I was serious. I was accepting a bad deal at the beginning of the year with the knowledge that by the end of the year, those same customers might come back and make me a lot of money. This kind of thinking involved a long-term mindset versus a short-term focus on individual transactions.

Sometimes patience on a personal level is both a byproduct of and a boon to the international experience. I spent a lot of time interacting with people who didn't speak English well or who were unfamiliar with American business practices. By slowing down, I could more effectively communicate. My manner of speaking became more efficient, and my ear tuned to the cadence of second-language English. I had foreign counterparts who spoke limited English, but with patience, I was able to clearly communicate their meaning to my team. I became almost a cultural broker, translating meaning and intent versus the words themselves.

BUSINESS PLANNING WITH PATIENCE

Developing a product or service for the local market takes a lot of time. You can't just storm in, guns blazing, and effectively sell whatever you sold in other parts of the world. You need to take time to fully understand the local market. What are people's needs, their problems, and their priorities?

While I was working for a company that sold many services and computer models, we developed customized products and services for the local Chinese market. China, like other emergent countries, had lower labor costs and unique local requirements. In most cases, product cycles were faster, and insider information was essential to understand and adhere to Chinese laws and regulations. If you understood the government regulations and standards, you were able to keep pace with the changing environment. We also needed to navigate an unfamiliar system to learn what made certain products thrive and others fail. We had to figure out who we could align ourselves with to overcome administrative roadblocks and make the process go smoothly.

PATIENCE IN NEGOTIATION

The Chinese and many countries in Southeast Asia are great negotiators. The art of bargaining was one of the most valuable things I picked up from living there. Some of it I learned at the street markets, where everybody wants a deal. It's almost a sport: it didn't matter if it was just five renminbi, it was about getting a better deal and a win. I still catch myself to this day trying to negotiate the best possible deal for anything, big or small.

This was also true on a larger business scale. You do not want to go into a negotiation in China unprepared. You need situational awareness: an understanding of the who, what, and where of the situation. Like restaurant manners and local habits, negotiation practices are just engrained in their minds. I picked up these several tactics by osmosis. I now feel like I can push the limits. The truth is that more people need to.

There's also a lot of patience that comes with negotiations. A great example is the "trade" dispute between the US and China. This is not anything new. It's been going on for decades and should have been solved a long time ago, but nobody wants to sit down and negotiate. It's reached a point now where the numbers are huge on both sides and the impacts are even greater. Nobody is willing to budge. The Chinese are great at being patient and will wait it out. They know we have elections every four years and we cycle through leaders. Our policies change all the time and are all over the place. They will simply wait for someone who they would rather deal with or who will be passive to their requests.

MAJOR TAKEAWAYS

On a personal and professional level, patience was one of the biggest virtues I developed abroad.

THE VIRTUES OF PATIENCE

What I learned about patience in China has helped me in major ways. I've become more understanding of people who've grown up in different environments and with different experiences. This empathy is something that is missing in a lot of companies in the US. It limits them and their ability to grow. It also limits the type of people they hire. Do you want people who all think the same, or do you want creative problem solvers?

GO WITH THE FLOW

Sometimes you just need to take a step back and let situations play out. The outcome might be positive, or it might not be, but with a little time, most things naturally reach a resolution. Watch, learn, and observe.

Dell had a direct sales model when we started. We let things get worse before they got better. Sometimes we would customize solutions locally to "test" them before we got support from the home office.

IT TAKES TIME TO BUILD TRUST

In the US, I've witnessed a limited amount of trust in the professional sphere. In Asia, a lot of relationships work only because of loyalty and trust. It made for better connections between colleagues and employees.

These ties, which will be discussed more in Lesson 8, take a lot of time to build. You simply can't rush personal connections.

MORE THAN ONE WAY TO GET THINGS DONE

With trust in others and a more open mind comes the realization that there is more than one way to get the same result. Being open to different ways of getting things done makes you more credible. It helps you learn new things and be more creative with solutions. Passing this on to other people typically improves communication and makes people less defensive.

NO IMMEDIATE GRATIFICATION

We live in a world today that emphasizes convenience. We want things done as quickly as possible. Instead of getting sucked into this mentality, it's important to take a step back and think about the big picture. Sometimes patience leads to much greater long-term gratification. Today, I question things that I wouldn't have in the past.

My self-reflection is more pointed. It makes me step back from the lure of instant gratification.

The startup world is all about producing and growing fast. Paradoxically, I found it easier to integrate into this fast-moving world because of my experience with effective long-term planning. It was about striking a balance between the plethora of ideas driving to produce and setting long-term goals and priorities. International experience wasn't completely necessary to achieve this, but it did speed up getting there.

ALWAYS BE CURIOUS

A generalized curiosity makes you a more informed person, which in turn helps you make better-informed decisions and fewer careless mistakes.

All my experiences have made me obsessed with learning new things. Some things you never find the answers to, but you try to understand the context and perspectives that can lead to solutions. Curiosity requires a certain level of patience because it is undirected, non-goal-oriented learning.

YOUR HIRING TEAM SHOULD BE INTERNATIONALLY AWARE

When I look at HR teams and hiring managers, I always want them to have international experience and awareness. This means finding people who have spent significant time living abroad or who grew up outside the United States.

Having these people in roles of talent acquisition will help you attract people from different parts of the world who have different mindsets and experiences. It will allow your company to grow and express new ideas and potentially expand into new markets. Without them, you may be able to achieve short-term results, but long term, it's going to hurt you.

With the world more connected and people having more access to travel and transportation, the future will see more of these internationally experienced people being effective in their roles. These more adaptable candidates will fill international positions across the board, from HR staff to business leadership.

LESSON 8

RESPECT AND EMPATHY

Although I spent a decade living in China, I must confess that I still only know a small fraction of what there is to know about the people, culture, and business environment of the country. It's such a complex place, and there are some experiences I will never fully understand simply because I'm not native Chinese. I know I still have much to learn, but staying in this learning mindset it a good place to be.

SOFT SKILLS THAT GET THINGS DONE

Soft skills are greatly needed in today's global business world. Respect and empathy are both extremely important for getting things done. Relationships require trust, something that the digital world tends to put up walls against.

The Chinese have several concepts that relate to this. *Xiao* (孝) refers to the importance of respecting your elders. The Chinese have a strict hierarchy based on age and experience, and it's important to recognize and respect that. As discussed in Lesson 1, this is true on both a personal and global level. It's important to recognize that China itself is an ancient culture compared to America's relatively new prominence.

It can take many years to establish the deep connections that come naturally to local businesses. Personal connections facilitate a lot of movement, whether they're people who went to school together or childhood friends. The phrase *zhong cheng* (忠诚) could mean "personal loyalty first," or "loyalty and honesty," and refers to the fact that the Chinese always put people they know and trust above people they don't. President Xi Jinping filled his cabinet with people he grew up with or had known for many years, regardless of their qualifications. One of the president's closest advisors grew up with him in a remote province after he fell out of favor during the Cultural Revolution. They lived together as small kids in exile after their fathers were removed from power. Their fathers eventually rose to senior-ranking politburo officials, which made Xi and his childhood friend princelings. It can take many years to earn that trust, but it's worth it when you do.

If you don't want to go down the bribery route, then you

have to start building connections, which takes time, patience, and effort. The Chinese saying for this is *ren qing* (人情), "appealing to the heart." It's asking someone a favor by appealing either to their vanity or their better nature, even though you are not able to reciprocate. Businesses could do this by pointing out a common shared goal, like improving environmental issues in China. The Chinese know there is a pollution problem in their country, and they don't want to destroy their land and air quality. Their leadership has made fixing this issue a priority, but they are still figuring out the right method, which leaves the door open for business opportunities.

The Chinese don't want to tear up their land and environment. They know there's a high degree of pollution in the country. The leadership has the common goal of fixing this issue but are still figuring it out. If you can find common ground in these places, your connections as a foreigner will grow, as will your opportunities.

LOCALIZE YOURSELF

My situation as a foreigner in China was somewhat unique in that, after a few years, I became a locally hired foreign national. I paid local taxes, submitted annual tax returns, participated in local thirteen-month bonus plans and supplemental wealth accumulation plans, and had local insurance. I was part of the Chinese pension plan, and if I'd stuck around for twenty years, I would have gotten a payout from the government. My kids went to international schools, but their classes were extremely diverse, with children from all over Europe and Asia.

This experience gave me a lot more insight into the complexities of life in China. For example, the renminbi isn't an open currency. Converting it to a foreign currency is a challenging process. You must show verification of your employment, residence permits, work permits, work contracts, and that you've paid your taxes, just to initiate an exchange. This is annoying on a personal level, but on a larger level, it's a major challenge that China faces. Over the next decade, they will need to open their financial institutions to make it easier for companies to enter the market and for capital to leave.

Another example is the healthcare system. My wife had our youngest son at an international hospital where they had foreign doctors and Chinese nationals educated in Western cultures. I couldn't believe how cheap the hospital bill was. It only cost about $3,000, compared to five times what we would have paid in the United States. Unfortunately, for locals, the healthcare system is quite expensive. While they do have centralized healthcare, it's not effective or efficient. There's also developing technology, so locals must travel to certain areas to get specific services. This is a challenge that the Chinese government is currently trying to tackle and a great area for international companies to make headway.

On the flip side, paying taxes was a different story. Since I was paid in the local currency, I was taxed by both China and the US. My tax form in China was one page, while my tax papers in the US totaled somewhere around seventy-five pages. My financial situation wasn't complex. I was just getting paid in a foreign currency. China stripped down the process into something much simpler. As an American, it's enviable.

A DEEPER CONNECTION

When I switched over from being an expat to being localized, it was a big deal. I could feel it in conversations with my employees, colleagues, and friends. The first four years I was paid in US dollars, but after 2010 I started getting paid in renminbi. The difference between locals and foreign workers is vast, and it brought people closer to me. I was participating in similar economic systems to them, which built up a coculture of empathy for our shared situation.

Contrary to what you might imagine, the laws in China are more favorable for workers than in the US. Each company has local contracts that fall under Chinese labor law. This means people can't be fired at will as in the US. Instead, they have "negotiable" severance. This is left up to the company and the individual. They can't just fire you. They must pay you at least an annual salary, plus bonus. If you're over the age of fifty-five and you've worked for the company for a certain number of years, they can't fire you without you agreeing to it, and with the severance money you deserve. The workers have a lot of leverage. This directly contradicts the foreign view of workers in China.

In China, there is a flat tax of 45 percent. You can mitigate this by submitting *fapiao*, or receipts for deductions, to your company's government representative monthly. Deductions change on a regular basis, depending on the government's agenda, but you could receive credit for everything from rent to transportation to eating out. These receipts are submitted through your employer and are reflected in your pay stub for the following month.

Prior to being localized, I had no idea about any of this. It deepened my connection with the country and my coworkers. It also deepened my respect for the individuals who dealt with these issues daily. I had to do the same things they did, and it helped me empathize. I could now talk directly with people and be understood and understand them more completely.

It didn't just help my interpersonal relationships; it also

helped me think more thoroughly about my business. I paid more attention to tax laws, deductions, and what the government's plans were. My deeper conversations with individuals led to better planning for the business. We could discuss initiatives that we foresaw two years down the road and where we could place people to be in situations that were beneficial to them. When I became managing director of the Shanghai site, I became more involved in the relationship between my employees, the company, and the local government. It brought me even closer to my workers.

THE IMPORTANCE OF SOCIALIZING

One of the ways our team built relationships was through shared dinners. Food is incredibly important in China. Sharing a meal together is a method of building camaraderie and making meaningful connections.

In the United States, coworkers may share meals or attend team-building events, but they are mostly seen as an obligation, not something to cherish or enjoy. Personal relationships between coworkers are often shallow. In China, eating or drinking together isn't about being dutiful, it's about making a cultural exchange and learning about one another. For example, I learned that the Chinese eat every part of the chicken, including the feet. It's a leftover practice from the many years of famine the country suffered. When food was scarce, you made use of everything and wasted nothing.

Sharing a meal or a drink is also a great way to unwind with employees. In Japan, we often did this through karaoke nights. I'd occasionally bring my wife and kids to dinner in China to build trust and make deeper, more personal connections.

Today, back in the US, I often bring my children to speaker and panel discussions on Asia so they can observe and mingle with new people. To me, it's a sign of respect.

CAREER BENEFITS OF ESTABLISHING TRUST

Initially in my career, I didn't take the time to build trust. As a result, people wrote me off and didn't give me second chances. When I developed as a person and began to build up a level of trust with my team members, it relaxed me. It also relaxed my employees because they could now see I wasn't just a two-year hire. I was there for the long haul. If I made mistakes, they were more accepting.

Furthermore, by promoting from within and moving individual contributors to manager positions, I could build more trust within my team. By giving them additional responsibilities and greater stakes in the company, it showed them that I was interested in their success and professional life. I watched my trusted employees grow in their careers.

My employees even began to protect me in certain ways. When my bosses or other foreigners came in, my colleagues would step in and help me out more. They'd highlight more effectively what I was doing, my management style, and how it worked. They gave me respect in front of my higher-ups because they knew I would do the same for them.

I was promoted several times during my career in China. Early on, I would overhear comments like "He's not one of us" or "He doesn't understand." That turned into "He gets it" and "He knows when to sing someone's praises." The Chinese are great at giving compliments. They connect with the ego and play to your soft side. The do it to flatter you but also to show their respect.

For example, when I had a boss come and meet with a local official, they showered my boss with compliments about his management style and how well he ran a program in the US. I recognized that they were just pumping him up so he'd be more open and less defensive. Early on, I thought it was genuine stuff, but as time goes on, you can see through the pageantry to the true meaning.

Becoming localized helped me to penetrate that fog

of ego-boosting and one-upmanship. I now could cut through the facade to ask important questions and get real answers. I could ask directly who was being paid off where. This disarmed people. It made them choose their words more carefully.

This building of empathy through respect and language also allows you to attract the right people to the right jobs. We call bosses who fly in occasionally to "review the business" seagulls. They fly in, shit, and fly out. Don't be a seagull!

MAJOR TAKEAWAYS

It takes a lot of time to develop cross-cultural under-standing, pick up foreign business skills, and experience perspective-changing aha moments.

INVESTING TIME

Working abroad is a learning process that could easily go on for an entire lifetime. Invest your time in understand-ing and respecting your host culture so that your mind is open to experiencing moments of clarity. An open mind is a gateway to further learning.

Developing the respect and empathy that empowers rela-tionships sometimes requires going native. You can't just be in and out or stay for a year or two. It takes a significant investment of time for the long-term benefit of yourself, the individuals you work with, and your business. This immersion experience is completely worth it. It cements your investment in the people and the country. It gives you more credibility.

BECOME AN AMBASSADOR

After being in China for a while, it became easier to articulate the details of the culture to people who didn't live there. I became a translator, not of what people were saying, necessarily, but of subtext and what they really meant. It was a way of bridging two cultures and expanding awareness of others so they could understand each other better.

In the US, it's always about getting things done the fastest. As a translator and "ambassador" for the culture, I was able to slow clients down and be a better promoter of constructive interactions and a better representative for my company.

BACK IN THE USA

Once you've earned that respect, the loyalty you receive in return is tremendous. It will even help you after you leave. If an issue pops up in your country of expertise, you can pick up the phone and quickly call the right person to get to the bottom of it. That's a huge boon.

Furthermore, with a better-developed sense of empathy, you become better positioned in your home country to serve a business. You can involve the right people in projects and bring in international experts on discussions. There's a tendency in the Western world to write off people who don't speak English well or at all. This is a grave error because these are the people whose input can potentially prove to be the most valuable. You don't want to have a committee made of people who all think the same way. It might take a little more patience, but it can yield bigger results.

CONCLUSION

I'd like to leave you with one last story.

You always hear rumors about strange or unsavory practice in China, like the trash-eating-pig incident I shared earlier. Later in my time in China, I witnessed another strange pig-related experience.

The Chinese are known for huge, lavish government functions, where thousands of guests dine on fancy food and fine wines. A few years ago, President Xi Jinping decided it was time to cut back on these banquets, which were an enormously expensive practice.

Pork is the most popular meat in China, and these banquets usually featured a lot of it. When the president makes a decision, it goes into effect immediately. When the government decided to rein in the spending, however, they still had outstanding contracts with pig farmers. When they found out they would no longer be paid for their pigs, the farmers got angry. They had a glut of pork on their hands and nowhere to sell it.

Out of frustration and anger, the farmers slaughtered the pigs and threw them into the Huangpu River, just upstream from Shanghai. These actions by the farmers certainly got the attention of government officials. The city had to deal with literally millions of bloated pigs floating down the river that supplied the city's drinking water.

There were constantly events and scandals like this happening during our time in China. Food and water safety was a constant concern for my family, and it took a lot of flexibility to adapt to this uncertain landscape. Sometimes the government seems to believe that "what you don't know won't hurt you."

Despite strange happenings like this one, I genuinely enjoyed my time living in China. It was an adventurous and wonderful experience that I couldn't fully appreciate until I learned to accept the culture, the people, and the government.

SEIZE OPPORTUNITIES ABROAD

As we move forward in this global economy, spending time abroad can help you develop the skills necessary to not only survive but thrive. International experience makes you a more patient, empathetic person. It helps you see past surface details to access deeper conclusions and cultural understanding.

People love to talk about the impacts of new technology and how it will shape the future, but they often overlook the soft skills that are every bit as important in developing and managing these new innovations. The only real way to develop those valuable skills is to spend a significant amount of time abroad, not just traveling but living, working, and learning.

There's a significant downside to businesses that don't hire people with international experience or who don't have programs in place for their people to spend time abroad. Obviously, the ramp becomes longer when conducting business in certain countries. Hire or develop people so that they can build bridges of understanding.

Long-term work abroad gives you a new perspective on the world around you. You can then take this self-awareness back home, where it becomes a valuable resource to any company. A lot of people in the United States have absolutely no idea what's going on outside the country. Your unique perspective can lead to more innovative ways of thinking and solving problems.

This type of heightened awareness makes you more open to trying new things and taking risks. My mind was trained to see things a certain way and to expect certain results. Ninety-five percent of the time, that's not necessarily what happened. By throwing away preconceived notions and expectations, you're more able to have an open mind. That state of openness is the key to succeeding in business.

Keep in mind that traveling internationally is not the same thing as actually working in an international environment. A lot of people would tell me they spent time in Shanghai, but when questioned further, it turns out they visited for a long weekend once. That's simply not enough time to understand what is going on over there. It takes time to cultivate a valuable understanding of another culture. As longtime expats like to say, you can't just be a seagull flying in and out; you must take the time to really integrate.

Although this book is primarily about my time abroad, I should note that I am a true patriot, and I love the country of my birth. If anything, living abroad has given me the distance to truly appreciate the things that make America great and the perspective to identify areas that need improvement.

The bottom line is if you have the opportunity to live abroad, take it. People make all kinds of excuses not to, but there really is no better time than right now. Yes, it may be challenging, but challenges can be good. Yes, you could go to Australia where everyone speaks English and the cultural barriers are low, but wouldn't it be even more rewarding to take on something really challenging? Sometimes hard is good. If you figure out the hard problems, everything else starts to look a lot easier.

WHAT ABOUT THE CHILDREN?

One of the most common excuses people give for turning down international experience is that they have a family. Kids are not an obstacle to relocating abroad. I went to China with two kids and came back with three and a dog!

Before we left, I did fret about "What are my kids going to get out of this?" But our time abroad was probably one of the greatest experiences I could have given them. They picked up all the same soft skills that I did. They were exposed to different cultures, religions, and perspectives. My kids learned even more because their minds were open from the get-go. They didn't have the same preconceptions I did, and as a result, they soaked up the new language and culture like sponges. Learning a language as a young child is so much easier than as an adult.

Observing my kids and how the culture affected them was fascinating. When we integrated back into the US, I could see that their minds and thought processes were different. They were more accepting and didn't judge as much. They were exposed to many cultures in an international school, many foods, and different religions.

Today, my kids are teenagers. Each of them wants to continue their global adventures.

My eldest wants to live outside the country and continue her experience learning multiple languages and traveling. My middle child constantly questions everything, like why US cities don't understand the value of mass transit. She relishes travel and exploration. My youngest will always have China written as his birthplace in his passport. I'm sure he will want to return to the land of his birth at some point.

Back in Texas, we find ourselves going to the Asian markets and picking out snacks like dried seaweed and fish because my kids love it. It's what they grew up on. Their change in perception was palpable. They knew a great deal more about the world than their peers back in Texas, who barely knew the map of their home state. That, to me, is a microcosm of how experience abroad compares to experience back home in the US.

START THINKING GLOBALLY

Now that you've had a chance to understand the eight lessons of international awareness, it's time to start putting that knowledge into action with your business. Businesses that overlook the importance of either hiring people with international experience or creating their own international programs are at risk of falling behind and missing valuable opportunities in emerging markets.

First, determine who has international experience or comes from abroad in your organization. These people possess unique talents that you may not be properly utilizing. Involve them in projects and committees, no matter what level in the organization they're at. Their mindset alone will be different and provide some significant influence on how to get stuff done.

For example, if you have someone who grew up in India who is now working in the US, they may be able to provide some interesting perspectives on products, product launches, management techniques, programs for rotation, and programs to develop skills. They grew up in a different environment and will have a different idea from the status quo.

To move forward in this new world, you need to have people from different backgrounds. They shouldn't all be Ivy Leaguers who were raised in a similar way and come from the same schools of thought. You should hire for different talents and bring people in who challenge the usual way of doing things. People who have gone through diverse experiences and have firsthand knowledge of some of the challenges that your business is trying to overcome are going to be the most valuable.

If you don't have people with international experience in your organization, then you need to change your hiring strategy. Look at your HR team and what their experiences are. Where do they come from? Are they hiring only a certain type of candidate? If so, evaluate if they are the right people for the job. They too should have international experience, especially if you're looking to expand into other parts of the world.

Another way to add people with international experience to your organization is to build your own international programs. There are many ways that you could do this.

You could test short-term international projects by sending small teams abroad to target countries. You could explore a more robust rotation program, consistently managed from the top, kind of like what the US military does. You could incentivize your employees to spend time abroad by offering financial incentives or the possibility of advancement. Or you could have paid programs where employees can learn new languages or study other cultures, either at home or at universities abroad. The possibilities are endless.

Don't just extend this opportunity to people in higher management positions. Encourage people from all levels of your organization to participate. It will allow individuals inside your organization to move more freely in their career objectives.

STRENGTH IN CHANGING MINDSETS

The old saying is true: what doesn't kill you makes you stronger. There are many joys and pains that you'll experience going abroad, but you're going to learn a lot more if you go through and come out of some of that pain. A lot of people are averse to taking risks. The truth is, if you take those risks, it typically makes you better. It may not happen immediately, but with time, you'll be stronger.

GLOSSARY OF TERMS

Laowai (老外)—A term the Chinese use to describe a foreigner and old friend, but also an alien, an outsider to the local culture. The word dates back thousands of years and was once used to describe foreign traders and ambassadors.

Qian xu (谦虚)—Humble.

Jian chi bu xie (坚持不懈)—Persistent to the end; never stop.

Hun luan (混乱)—Can be translated into chaotic, confused, disorderly. China's system is designed to prevent chaos and disorder.

Zhen (震)—The experience of dealing with shocking events; shaking.

Zhen han (震撼)—Strong emotional impact on people.

Ren (忍)—The patience of the job. This refers to the Chinese tendency to tackle tasks with carefully thought out precision that often comes from long and slow deliberation and contemplation. Endure hardship to get things done. Calm, persistent, even if it's tough.

Ren qing (人情)—Appealing to the heart; asking someone a favor by appealing either to their vanity or their better nature, even though you are not able to reciprocate in the immediate future.

Xiao (孝)—The importance of respecting your elders. The Chinese have a strict hierarchy based on age and experience, and it's important to recognize and respect that.

Zhong cheng (忠 诚)—Loyalty, honesty; personal loyalty first.

Ling huo (灵活)—Doing things flexibly (actions).

ACKNOWLEDGMENTS

When I started down the road toward writing this book, I had no idea how to turn my many ideas and stories into something worth reading. I just wanted to share my opinions and observations. Of course, I had dreams of being the world's best-selling author, winning a Pulitzer or maybe a Nobel Prize. All of that was just my ego talking.

As I went through the process, collected my thoughts, and asked people for help, I realized that by reflecting on the past, I could create inspiration for the future. I also realized that my real inspiration was the people I'm lucky enough to have in my life. Without these people, I would not be here today.

I would like to thank my parents, who not only put up with all my hoodlum activities, young and old, but established a core set of values, work ethic, and responsibility in me. To my mother, who has always been a source of motivation, understanding, and patience. My father, who instilled in me situational awareness, trust, and loyalty. Take care of what you have and always be grateful for being alive. You have patiently taught me well.

To my wife, Shelley, for accepting the bad and bringing out the good in me. For experiencing all the adventures as a team and the joy of sharing those memories together. I would not be here today without her. She has put up with my visions of greatness, my absurd thoughts, and my dreams with only patience and support. For this I will be forever grateful.

To my wonderful children who have inspired me to learn and grow. My son, Zach, who will forever have China as his place of birth on his passport. He has that gift of exploring, learning, and awareness at a young age, which will place him for greatness in the future. My daughter Carly, who inspires me through her sense of commitment, no-fear attitude, and street smarts. There are no mistakes, only learning opportunities. My eldest daughter Reese, who continues to shock the world with greatness: her natural ability to lead, her conviction for learning, and her balanced mind. The world awaits. Watching and observing all my children leaves me in awe for what they will accomplish. I am humbled.

To the entire Scribe team, who helped piece this together. From the first conversation with Tucker Max, who told me, "Call me back when you know why you want to write a book." To Karla Bynum, who patiently worked through the outline in a way my mind never works. To Stephanie Yoder, who encouraged me to dig deeper and keep momentum. To James Timberlake, my publishing manager, who has only words of wisdom, direct feedback, and a positive flow of energy. And last, to Erin Tyler for the best damn cover design in the world!

To all the people I have worked with in the US and Asia for making these experiences real. I would like to thank my China friends and colleagues for teaching me the importance of respect, loyalty, and hard work. Without their openness, mentorship, and patience, these learnings would not be possible. Special thanks to Jilly Guo, who supported me throughout most of my time in China. She is an inspiration for commitment, dedication, and patience. This book would not have been possible without lifelong friendships, laughter, and spirit.

Always be curious.

Seek gratitude.

Everything happens for a reason.

ABOUT THE AUTHOR

TYLER JOHNSON grew up in a military family, which meant starting over in a new location every two years. After several attempts at college, he graduated with a degree in psychology—not business.

He began as a temp employee for Dell, making just nine dollars an hour, before working his way up to an executive position and eventually leading a $1 billion Asian business unit. During his decade as managing site director for Dell in Shanghai, he traveled throughout China, India, Southeast Asia, Australia, and Japan.

Tyler has worked with some of Asia's largest tech firms and has more than twenty years of experience with Fortune 50 executive leadership across the US and Asia. He continues to work in the technology industry and lives in Austin, Texas, with his wife and three kids.